THE WEIGHT

OF YOUR

WORDS

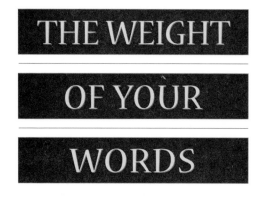

THE WEIGHT
OF YOUR
WORDS

*Measuring the
Impact of
What You Say*

Joseph M. Stowell

MOODY PRESS
CHICAGO

CONTENTS

INTRODUCTION 9

1. A WORD'S WORTH 13
   The "Problem" Tongue Exposed

2. TO TELL THE TRUTH 23
   Beguilement, Deceit, Lying, and False Witness

3. MALICIOUSLY SPEAKING 35
   Gossip and Slander—Catastrophic Cousins

4. THE EGO IN OUR MOUTHS 47
   Boasting, Flattery, and Exaggeration

5. CROSS WORDS 57
   Murmuring and Contentious Words

6. EXPLETIVES DELETED 67
   Using God's Name in Vain and Sensuous Speech

7. HEART TALK 77
   Your Tongue Reflects Your Spirit

8. SPEAKING OUT FOR NUMBER ONE 87
   Push Your Pride Aside

9. DEFUSING ANGER 97
   Douse the Fire in Your Tongue

10. PATIENCE APPLIED 107
    Good Words for Bad Deeds

11. THE TRUST-LOVE LIFE 119
    Conquer Fear with Love

12. APPLES OF GOLD 131
    A Commitment to Positive Speech

STUDY GUIDE 141

Talk shows are just the tip of the iceberg, but they represent a significant arena of verbal venom. Some programs try to feature the most foul and outlandish topics to pander to the lowest basic instincts of their listeners. Others, even the reputable ones, spotlight people who may or may not have their facts straight. Yet people in the audience tend to take everything they hear as truth.

Consider also the recent rise in "trash talk" in the world of sports. Some of the top athletes in the world want you to *know* they're the top athletes, so they master verbal putdowns of their opponents. Then along come young and impressionable kids (and not-so-young adults) who idolize these athletes as their heroes. And even if they can't emulate the athletic prowess of the players, they can surely mimic the trash talk. It's not unusual to walk past a playground and hear even the youngest kids boasting, spewing profanity, hurling insults, and otherwise saying things that will draw attention to themselves.

Another increasingly widespread problem is "road rage." More and more commuters are becoming impatient with their fellow drivers, and sometimes it takes only the slightest provocation—either real or perceived—to set them off. Perhaps you've read stories about people who have been severely beaten or even killed because of a comment they made to another driver.

It's easy to notice these flagrant violations of *word power.* What is more important is the recgonition of the subtle aspects of the impact of our words on significant relationships as well as our talk to those who come in and out of our lives on a casual basis. A committed follower of Christ cannot fail to notice and deal with verbal categories like gossip, slander, deceit, boasting, and beguilement. God meant that our words be used to help and heal. Tackling this transition is critical to our success in every arena of life. A raging river can be destructive and demolish everything in its path. But if the river is channeled to turn a grist mill or produce electricity, the same power becomes beneficial and desirable. The "energy" produced by our words can be a benevolent gift to others. But if we don't learn to channel it, the impact may knock them off their feet emotionally.

Something else has changed since the first edition of this book was published. The recent dearth of productive words is getting noticed, so they are becoming a desired commodity. A poll was taken of a hundred and fifty executives to determine what they deemed the most critical qualities in a job candidate. In 1990 the most desired characteristic was "verbal skills." It was clear that words were important. Yet the results of the same poll released in 1997 showed a surprising shift in thinking. The category of "verbal skills" had dropped to third on the list. Enthusiasm was second. But the *most* desired traits for employees today are honesty and integrity. It seems that it is becoming less important *how well* you say something and more crucial to be trustworthy in *what* you say. The poll noted that people who interview potential employees now spend significant time evaluating a job candidate's character and integrity.

As James wrote, "If anyone does not stumble in what he says, he is a perfect man, able to bridle the whole body as well" (3:2). That is the goal I want to strive toward. Maybe you're already there. But if not, I hope this book will guide you and help you on your way.

the most problems for us. When used appropriately, our words have the power to heal, encourage, help, and teach. On the other hand, words can also confuse, embarrass, and hurt.

Here is one man's testimony of the destructive potential that words possess:

> My junior high school had scheduled its annual operatic production. Talented students were quick to try out for the various parts. I was not so certain of my abilities and had decided that singing in an operetta wasn't really for me.
>
> Then Mrs. Wilson, my music teacher, asked me to try out. It was not a coveted role, but it *did* have three solos.
>
> I am certain that my audition was only mediocre. But Mrs. Wilson reacted as if she had just heard a choir of heavenly angels. "Oh, that was just beautiful. It was perfect. You are just right for the role. You will do it, won't you?" I accepted.
>
> When the time came for the next year's operetta, most of the students who had played the leads the year before had graduated. And Mrs. Wilson had transferred to another school. In her place was a rather imposing figure who had an excellent singing voice and a sound knowledge of music theory.
>
> As the tryouts began, I was ready. I felt confident that my talent was just what the operetta needed. With approximately 150 of my peers assembled, I knew everything would go well.
>
> But if I live for an eternity I will never forget the words spoken on that day. When my audition was completed, the teacher asked, "Who told you you could sing?"
>
> The timid youth of a year earlier was suddenly reborn. I was totally destroyed. Harsh words are bad enough under any circumstances. To a young idealistic boy, they can be devastating. From the time those six words were stated, it took eight years and the coaxing of my fiancée before my voice was raised in song again.

You can probably recall similar instances from your own past where a few words—either positive or negative—made a significant difference in your life. Words have tremendous weight. Recent studies tend to disprove the saying many of us grew up with: "Sticks and stones may break my bones, but names will never hurt me." Adults polled said they had gotten over most of the *physical* pains of childhood. But many had never fully recovered from the hurtful words, names, and labels that had been placed on them. Physical wounds heal, as is evidenced from the scars we carry. But verbal wounds frequently refuse to close, oozing pain and keeping us tender and vulnerable.

In spite of all of Job's physical and emotional suffering, the verbal jabs of his so-called friends made his situation even worse. He challenged one of them: "How long will you torment me and crush me with words?" (Job 19:2).

We must be constantly aware that our words carry an impact. They affect our children, our students, our spouses, our friends, our neighbors, and our business associates. That's why God holds me accountable for "every careless word" (Matthew 12:36). Yet controling the words that come out of my mouth is a huge challenge.

For one thing, the stress of everyday encounters gets the better of us. We quickly say things we don't really mean. In addition, most of us are exposed to negative patterns of speech on a daily basis. From the demeaning words of an angry boss to the crude language of prime-time television, from sarcastic conversation with a neighbor to careless chatter among Christians, many of us have regular exposure to corrupted communication. The problem is that such verbal habits are highly contagious. Unfortunately, our tongues often recycle the input and, to our chagrin, the destructive words are out of *our* mouths before we know it—occasionally in front of people who can't believe what they're hearing!

Whether the reason is unintentional confusion, careless destruction, survival in chaos, or subconscious submission to environmental patterns of speech, inappropriate words are always destructive. Having a tongue is like having dynamite in our dentures—it's got to be reckoned with. It influences three major dimensions of our lives: our relationship with God, our relationship with those we treasure the most, and even our relationship with ourselves.

God's Word describes the tremendous task we face.

the potential to quickly kill a relationship, paralyze love, poison minds, destroy faith, stain purity, and deface reputations.

PRINCIPLE 5: THE TONGUE
TENDS TO PROMOTE A DOUBLE STANDARD

"With [the tongue] we bless our Lord and Father, and with it we curse men, who have been made in the likeness of God; from the same mouth come both blessing and cursing. My brethren, these things ought not to be this way. Does a fountain send out from the same opening both fresh and bitter water? Can a fig tree, my brethren, produce olives, or a vine produce figs? Neither can salt water produce fresh" (James 3:9–12).

Someone has said that most tongues are tied in the middle, wagging at both ends. Perhaps this was the image in Paul's mind when he warned Timothy to avoid positioning "double-tongued" men as church leaders (1 Timothy 3:8). It's amazing how we can verbally poison other people all the way to church, but as soon as we pull into the parking lot we begin to speak out of the pious side of our mouths. Then we hardly finish singing the doxology until we start complaining again. "My brethren, these things ought not to be this way."

Even nature doesn't act so incongruously. It is impossible for wells to produce both salt and freshwater, or for fig trees to bear olives! We would be utterly disappointed to expect a cold drink of pure water, only to draw up a bucket full of salty and undrinkable seawater. Similarly, God must be disappointed whenever His "new creatures" (see 2 Corinthians 5:17) continue to issue "old words."

KEEPING OUR TONGUES IN CHECK

In these five principles James categorizes the dark and shifty potential of the tongue. The first step toward victory is to permit these truths to penetrate our minds and hearts. The warning is clear: A transformed tongue must be a top priority for those committed to spiritual growth.

James's warning, however, takes on added weight when we realize that many Christians are insensitive to the problems of destructive speech. We excuse one another with a number of rationalizations. For example, perhaps you have heard someone say something derogatory about another person, yet accompany the damaging statement with one of the following disclaimers:

- "Well, it's the truth, isn't it?"
- "If they didn't want people to talk, they never should have done it."
- "Let me share this with you so we can pray more intelligently."
- "I heard this from a reliable source, or I wouldn't be repeating it."

This desensitization process opens the floodgates to communication sins. By making careless communication an acceptable part of our lives, we strive for spiritual maturity while exempting the tongue from the process. Yet the word-sparks that fly from an untamed tongue can leave an entire life (or lives) in ashes. Until we get serious about bringing our tongues under the control of the Holy Spirit, our churches, schools, homes, friendships, and relationships with God will all be victimized.

Sins such as beguilement, deceit, lying, and false witness need to be understood from God's point of view. Social sins of the tongue, including gossip and slander, must be checked. Verbal ego trips, such as boasting, flattery, and exaggeration, are clearly out of bounds. The cancer of a murmuring, contentious tongue needs to be removed. Expletives that violate the dignity of God's name and our sensitivity to moral purity must be deleted.

The following chapters will go into further detail in all these areas. But first let me provide a recent illustration of how serious we need to be about controlling our speech. A favorite sportswriter of mine once analyzed a fine levied on a local baseball manager for verbally chewing out the commissioner. His column defended the manager by saying, "After all, they were just words." At the time I thought, *Just words?*

This erosion of trust and confidence weakens every relationship into which nontruth is injected. Homes are victimized, governments become suspect, media information is viewed with skepticism, and business relationships wear the shrouds of suspicion. No relationship can survive, let alone succeed, if it is based on that which is false.

SPIRITUAL CONSEQUENCES

Scripture emphasizes the serious spiritual consequences of tampering with the truth. A moratorium on lying is included in the Ten Commandments (Exodus 20:16). A lying tongue is included in the list of things God detests (Proverbs 6:17). Liars are included with those whose lives will be judged in the lake of fire (Revelation 21:8). God desires for truth to dwell within us (Psalm 51:6). But *why* is truth so important to God?

For one thing, *truth aligns us with God.* God's intense concern for truthfulness centers on His very nature. He is a "God of truth" (Psalm 31:5). God cannot lie (Titus 1:2). Jesus Christ is "full of grace and truth" (John 1:14). The Holy Spirit is the "Spirit of truth" and His mission is to guide us into the truth (14:17; 16:13). All the ways of God are true (Psalm 25:10). The truth is the basis of our worship (John 4:24). Therefore, a commitment to truth aligns us with God, His nature, and His mode of operation. It is a matter of fellowship.

Second, *we are redeemed to reflect God's character.* Our very purpose in existing as God's children is to be conformed to the image of His Son (Romans 8:29). When we participate in falsehood, we abort the purpose of our redemption and tarnish the reflection of His glory through us. If God is truth, then we too must portray truth to accurately reflect God's image in our lives.

And third, *truth-telling is a matter of submission to God's will.* God's Word commands us to speak the truth—regardless of the cost. "A righteous man hates falsehood" (Proverbs 13:5). Paul wrote, "Do not lie to one another" (Colossians 3:9). Nowhere in Scripture does God grant exemption from these commands. They are absolute. Our consciences cannot be clear before God and our joy cannot be full if we get involved with falsehoods.

Many people have attempted to categorize the distortion of truth. For our study, let's look at four categories we need to understand.

BEGUILEMENT

This is the tendency to reach a wrong conclusion and perhaps even share our false assumptions with all who will listen. Our quickness to jump to wrong conclusions is a subtle trap because it victimizes us when we have no intention to be deceived or to deceive.

I was especially aware of this problem when I was a pastor. One morning while leaving for the office, I noticed that someone had thrown a beer can on my front lawn. I picked it up, tossed it in the garbage can, and drove away without giving it much thought. But on the way to work, the thought hit me: *What will the garbage men think? A beer can tumbling out of the minister's garbage can?* Though I had done nothing improper, I realized how easy it would be for someone to reach a wrong conclusion and judge me guilty without a trial.

You can't always prevent others from reaching false conclusions about you, but you *can* become more aware of your own assumptions about others. I recall discovering some money missing from the church office. Immediately, a suspect's name and face came to mind. I caught myself mentally degrading the person, planning how I would confront him, and wondering who I should tell so they could "pray about the situation." I felt my anger building. My judgmental spirit had pronounced the verdict. As the staff discussed the "case of the missing cash," I was quick to indict the guilty party. My spirit had developed a negative focus, and just thinking about "the thief" aroused a scornful response in me.

Then it was as though the Holy Spirit tapped me on the shoulder and said, "What if you are wrong? Do you have all the facts?" It occurred to me that I had not an ounce of proof. Even our secular system of justice proclaims a man

- Professors who selectively choose statistics to prove a
  point.

Deceit is a prevalent reality in our society. It is a destroyer
of trust. It is a menace to stable, growing relationships.

Legal restraints such as "truth-in-advertising," "truth-in-
lending," and "truth-in-testimony" demonstrate how prevalent deceit is in our way of life. The result of the undermin-
ing of our confidence through deceit in media, government,
business, politics, and tragically, even in the church, has been
labeled a "credibility gap."

The writer of Proverbs says, "Bread obtained by falsehood is sweet to a man, but afterward his mouth will be filled
with gravel" (20:17). Deceit is the sign of a wicked heart
(12:20).

Both beguilement and deceit tamper with, twist, and dis-
tort the truth. Lying, on the other hand, is the direct communication of nontruth.

LYING

Coconut has always been one of my weaknesses. For me,
there is a direct connection between coconut and my early
impressions about lying. One day when I was young, I came
home from school and discovered a bag of shredded
coconut in the kitchen cupboard. I succumbed to the temptation and ate it. How was I to know my mother intended to
use it for a cake she was baking that night? Upon discovering
that her cupboards had been vandalized, my mother called
my two sisters and me to the kitchen and demanded a confes-
sion. My sisters swore their innocence. I, of course, followed
suit.

When my father came home, he sat all of us down in the
living room. We each affirmed our innocence again. Mark
Twain once said, "The principle difference between a cat and
a lie is that a cat has only nine lives." Well, I was at nine and
counting when my dad opened his Bible and read that liars
have their place in the lake of fire (Revelation 21:8). That
did it. I could hold out no longer, and I sheepishly confessed.

Since that day I have had a deep respect for the seriousness of lying. I learned that "those who cook up stories usually find themselves in hot water." It wasn't until later in life, however, that I discovered *why* lying was such a serious matter to God. Scripture relates several realities about a lying tongue that should give every believer cause for concern.

Lying is the base of Satan's strategy. In Genesis 3, not only did Satan *deceive* Eve about God's goodness, but he also *lied* to her about God and His Word. He told her, "You surely shall not die!" (Genesis 3:4). That was a clear communication of nontruth. God had said, "In the day that you eat from [the tree] you shall surely die" (2:17). Lying was a central part of Satan's strategy.

It is not surprising that nontruth is still Satan's main method of operation today. He has pervaded our culture with the lie that there are no consequences to sin. His system tells us that wealth and possessions will make us happy. He lies to us about God by suggesting, "If God is good, why did He permit your parents to divorce? Why is there so much suffering?"

His lies are abundant:

- Be as good as you can, and you'll go to heaven. Just be sincere.
- Mankind is the result of a chance evolutionary process.
- Success can be measured by wealth, cars, and houses.
- Freedom is found in doing anything you want to do.

Lying is the strength of Satan's system. Not only does *he* lie, but his desire is that *we* will lie as well. When we lie, we imitate Satan rather than God. That's exactly what Christ inferred when He said to the Pharisees who had lied about Him, "You are of your father the devil, and you want to do the desires of your father. He was a murderer from the beginning, and does not stand in the truth because there is no truth in him. Whenever he speaks a lie, he speaks from his own nature, for he is a liar and the father of lies" (John 8:44).

Nontruth is the language of the world's system. James warns us that friendship with the world is hostility toward God and that anyone who chooses to be a friend of the world becomes an enemy of God (James 4:4).

Lying is part of the believer's past. Lying is a product of the flesh that we should leave behind as we mature spiritually. "Do not lie to one another, since you laid aside the old self with its evil practices, and have put on the new self who is being renewed to a true knowledge according to the image of the One who created him" (Colossians 3:9–10). Our newness aligns us with Christ and with His truth. Anyone who enjoys fellowship with God "speaks truth in his heart" and "does not slander with his tongue" (Psalm 15:2–3).

Even though lying is the base of Satan's strategy and a part of our spiritual past, it lingers as an ever-present tendency within us. We are frequently tempted to lie in order to serve ourselves or to serve others.

Why do we lie so readily? Lying is a quick and easy way to gain advantage, protection, and promotion of personal interests. We lie to get people's attention and have them think more highly of us. We lie to get rich or to get elected. We lie to protect our reputations. We lie to escape punishment. Most lies are dedicated servants of self.

In my first pastorate, the Sunday school superintendent reminded me to order the Sunday school books so they would be on hand for the new quarter. I promised I would, but I promptly forgot. The next Sunday as I walked through the foyer, I met the superintendent. He asked if I had ordered the materials. In a flash, I lied to protect my reputation. After all, how could I, the pastor, have forgotten? How could I be so careless with his needs? As I walked on to my office, I was annoyed at how quickly I had responded with a lie. It wasn't premeditated—it was instinctive and automatic. Self-interest was still alive and well in my being. I also found myself overcome with guilt.

As I settled in at my desk, the Holy Spirit urged me to clear up the matter before I preached. I was in turmoil. Could I admit to the superintendent that I had lied? Could I live without admitting it? The flesh and the Spirit were waging all-out internal war (Galatians 5:17). The superintendent would never know the difference if I didn't tell him. I could call the next morning and have the order rushed. If it didn't arrive in time, I could always blame the publishing house. On the other hand, if I admitted my falsehood, my credibility would be destroyed.

Ultimately my rationalizations proved to be of no avail. I knew I was wrong. I knew I had to confess—to God and to the superintendent. If I didn't, my relationship with him would be tainted with guilt and fear. I knew that lying, even if undiscovered, drives a wedge between the best of friends. If I didn't make it right, my preaching would be from the heart of a hypocrite harboring known sin.

Thankfully, upon confessing what I had done, I found the man to be graciously forgiving. My spirit was free—I had won back a friend and deepened a relationship.

A greater challenge to our commitment to truth is telling lies as a form of protection. At first this may seem to be a valid exception to the righteous goal of truthfulness. We've all heard the war stories of Jewish children who were asked by the Nazi soldiers if their parents were home. From the weighty consideration of that kind of situation to the common "social lies" that keep everyone smiling in spite of how they really feel, we tend to excuse certain lies.

Admittedly, it is sometimes hard to apply the truth tactfully. What do you say when you're expected to comment on a newborn, red, wrinkled baby in the hospital? How do you respond when asked to admire a new dress, hat, or tie that should have been left on the store shelves? In such cases, we often tell "little white lies." The phrase itself is a contradiction; lying is never little and it is always a part of darkness! As someone once said, "Those who are given to white lies soon become color blind."

This is not to say that we are to express truth brutally. God's Word commands us to speak the truth *in love* (Ephesians 4:15). The truth must be accompanied by mercy, gentleness, understanding, and grace. There is no virtue in glorifying

As a result, an innocent man was stoned to death and a sulking king got his garden (1 Kings 21:1–16). At the crucifixion of Christ, the high priest brought in two "false witnesses" to testify against the Lord (Matthew 26:60–61). The verbal sin of "bearing false witness" is a serious offense before God. In fact, it was this term God used when He included a prohibition against lying in the Ten Commandments (Exodus 20:16).

This sin is offensive because it strikes injury, often irreparable, to innocent people, their reputations, and their families. It is a violent use of the tongue. It had the power to kill Naboth and to crucify Christ. It's not surprising that Proverbs 19:5 says, "A false witness will not go unpunished, and he who tells lies will not escape."

Beguilement, deceit, lying, and false witness are all methods of Satan to defeat God's glory in us and through us. It is through these patterns of falsehood that he enlists us into the network of his "nontruth system."

Nontruth is part of every sin that Satan promotes. Whether it be lying to cover marital unfaithfulness or the destruction of a godly reputation by beguilement, whether using deceit to gain an unjust business advantage or bearing false witness to carry out some selfish scheme, tampering with the truth supports, promotes, and protects the welfare of sin. Can you think of a single sin where nontruth isn't a natural by-product or companion? It is the lifeblood of Satan's system.

In 1995, a bill was passed in Arizona to prevent people from spreading lies about vegetables. Known as the "veggie hate crimes bill," it allows farmers to sue anyone who distributes false information about Arizona farm products with malicious intent. If only more of us would consider lying about (and to) *other people* as serious! It seems ironic that some of us may be more concerned about our vegetables than we are about the lives of those we come into contact with every day.

Oliver Wendell Holmes expressed it well: "Sin has many tools, but a lie is the handle that fits them all."

3

MALICIOUSLY SPEAKING

Gossip and Slander—Catastrophic Cousins

They call them urban legends—stories that are widely purported to be true but are never proven. There's one about a woman who smuggled back a Chihuahua on her return from Mexico, only to discover weeks later that it was a large rat. Another is about a man who took his choking German shepherd to the vet, who found part of a finger in the dog's throat. The man rushed home to find a burglar passed out in a corner. They are great stories—tall tales for our generation!

My first encounter with urban legends came several years ago. I heard that someone in our church had a couple of elderly aunts who wanted to visit New York City. They had been warned what an evil place it was. With the possibility of robbery, mugging, rape, or even murder lurking around every corner, they were advised to stay home.

Undaunted, the two ladies went anyway. After checking in to a fancy downtown hotel, they promptly made their way to the elevator. The door opened and there stood a large, stern-looking man wearing sunglasses and a white suit. A leashed Doberman pinscher stood at his side. The ladies glanced nervously at each other and got in. No sooner had the elevator doors closed, than the man commanded, "Sit!" The ladies both sank to the floor. When the elevator stopped, the man and his dog made their way past the sitting spinsters, who then continued their ride up.

Upon checking out of the hotel, the ladies found that their room had been paid for. A note was attached to the bill. It read, "Ladies, you gave me the best laugh of my life. Your room's on me! Reggie Jackson."

Convinced the story was true, I took great delight in sharing it with friends. A group of professional baseball players thought it was the funniest thing they had ever heard. Then one evening as I told it to a group of couples, someone said, "I just read about that in *People* magazine. It's a rumor. Reggie Jackson emphatically denies it. He never wears white suits!" To say the least, I was embarrassed. I had been caught red-handed with a rumor in my mouth.

More devastating, however, are rumors that destroy people. Recently, it was discovered that the thirteen-year-old daughter of a Florida hospital clerk had printed out a list of her mother's patients with their phone numbers. She was arrested for allegedly calling the people and telling them they had tested positive for the AIDS virus. One of the people she phoned had Caller ID and police were able to determine what had happened. The girl said it was just a prank, but one of the people she called was a married sixty-year-old woman who would have killed herself if family members hadn't prevented her from getting her father's gun.

Rumors, whether true or false, are devastating for many reasons—one being that they are irretrievable. I recall the story of a young man during the Middle Ages who went to a monk and said, "I've sinned by telling slanderous tales about someone. What should I do?"

The monk replied, "Put a feather on every doorstep in town."

The young man did just that. He then returned to the monk, wondering if there was anything else he should do.

"Go back and pick up all those feathers," the monk told him.

The young man replied excitedly, "That's impossible! By now the wind will have blown them all over town!"

Said the monk, "So have your slanderous words become impossible to retrieve."

THE SELF-CENTERED SIX

Rumors are the vehicles that turn life into a demolition derby, and gossip and slander are the tracks on which they travel. The tracks of gossip and slander are littered with careless, idle chatter as well as malicious, intentional bad-mouthing. Where does the fuel for this demolition derby come from? Malicious speech comes from the central source of all sin—the promotion of self. Gossip and slander feed on our natural self-orientation in at least six ways.

First is the self-orientation of *curiosity*. Some of us look for and listen to "news" just because of our natural curiosity. Obviously, this can be constructive. A curiosity to know God and His will is a spiritual plus. Theologians, scientists, inventors, and others depend on curiosity to make advancements in their fields. Yet, if our curiosity includes seeking, bearing, and disseminating harmful information, then we have moved into the destructive aspect of curiosity. It's not by accident that 1 Timothy 5:13 links busybodies (people whose curiosity has gone wild) with gossips (those who share what their unchecked curiosity has discovered) in the same negative context.

The same verse provides a second self-centered source of gossip and slander: *idleness*. Paul explains that people with time on their hands may be prone to malicious speech. In writing about certain widows, Paul says they are "idle, as they go around from house to house." Today we don't even have to make the effort to wander from house to house. Idleness causes many people to pick up a cellular phone or sit down to visit their favorite chat rooms on the Internet. Gossip and slander no longer require physical exertion. People who are slothful may easily become slanderous. In contrast, people who are constructively involved with their own responsibilities have little time to be nosy about the responsibilities of others.

Third, *a desire to be the center of attention* often is the impetus for slander or gossip. It's an ego stroke to have everyone listening intently when we speak, so we learn the right phrases to captivate others:

- "Did you hear?"
- "Well, I really shouldn't say this, but..."
- "Can you keep a secret?"

Some of us feed on any kind of attention. Unfortunately, it often comes at the expense of others.

Fourth, *the opportunity to elevate ourselves over others* frequently stimulates negative speech. If I can say something derogatory about you, I feel better about myself (or at least I can hope to influence the person I'm talking to). As Will Durant said, "To speak ill of others is a dishonest way of praising ourselves."

Fifth, malicious words are often spawned by *bitterness*. Selfishly withholding forgiveness opens the door to a vengeful spirit, and slander is a tool of revenge. The slander we pour out against those who have hurt us is the natural vent of our hostile spirit. In fact, unresolved bitterness will be transferred to other situations that remind us of the events which angered us in the first place. Until we rid ourselves of bitterness, all aspects of our lives are likely to be characterized by slander.

Sixth, we are prone to speak of negative things because *it soothes our own anxieties*. Misery still loves company. That's why bad news moves by express while good news hardly gets down the track. Watch any network news program and calculate the percentage of good-news stories in contrast to the bad-news leads. Good news about others heightens our anxieties about our own problems.

In God's Word, several terms are used to describe this destructive pattern of speech, but there are two primary categories. The first is *idle chatter demeaning another's integrity and reputation* (1 Tim. 5:13; 6:20; 2 Tim. 2:16). This category of verbal misuse is not always malicious in its intent, but it is always damaging. The concept is frequently translated in Scripture as *whisper* or *gossip* (Psalm 41:7; Proverbs 20:19). The second category includes the *intentional, malicious communication of bad reports*. This concept is normally translated *slander* (Psalm 31:13; Jeremiah 9:4; 2 Corinthians 2:20).

GOSSIP

R. G. LeTourneau, the owner of a large earth-moving equipment company, often told this story: "We used to have a scraper known as the Model G. Somebody asked one of our salesmen what the 'G' stood for. The salesman was pretty quick on the trigger and replied, 'Well, I guess the G stands for gossip, because like gossip, this machine moves a lot of dirt, and moves it fast!'"

Both the Hebrew and Greek words for gossip are picturesque. One of the Old Testament words refers to "going about from one to another" (Proverbs 11:13) and is the source of our word *talebearing.* Another Hebrew word presents the concept of "whispering that is damaging" (Proverbs 16:28; 18:8; 26:20, 22).

The New Testament word also deals with the aspect of whispering. One lexicographer describes it as "secret attacks on a person's character." The pronunciation of the Greek word for gossip begins with the sound *p-s-s-s,* which is often how we characterize hushed communication.

Scripture always presents whispering in a negative context. The word denotes confidential communication, non-public information, exclusivism, secretive behavior, and shame. In the Bible, whispering becomes a figurative expression for the sin of gossip, which unfortunately is not always done in a whisper.

God's Word teaches that a person who gossips is untrustworthy and cannot keep a secret (Proverbs 11:13). Gossips often betray confidential information. Their information is not worthy of trust because the source usually tends to add "frills" to the story to make it more interesting.

A person who gossips is to be avoided (20:19). Hearing gossip adds unneeded information to our mental notebooks. These negative thoughts give Satan a foothold in our lives. Hearing often results in telling—for some people, "gossip in" soon becomes "gossip out."

Gossip adds fuel to the fire created by the tongue (26:20). Gossips have a great ability to keep division and strife at a fever pitch by sharing bits of information that are difficult to ignore or forget (18:8; 26:22). The "juicy morsels" stay with us, permanently staining our perceptions of and appreciation for those about whom we are hearing. The vicious chain of gossip continues until it finally comes up against someone willing to stop spreading information about feuding factions and start praying. Only then will the fire die down.

Gossip separates the closest of friends (16:28). When you hear gossip about a friend, it begins to drive a wedge between the two of you. It builds a barrier of suspicion and doubt. Conversely, if your friend gossips to you about someone else, you begin to doubt his or her loyalty. After all, if he gossips *to* you, maybe he will gossip *about* you.

A gossiper disqualifies himself for fellowship with God and shows his lack of knowledge of God (Psalm 15:1–3; Romans 1:28–30). When we are victims of gossip, we need to realize that God knows, that He cares, and that He can deal with the situation. We can find peace only when we leave the situation to "Him who judges righteously" (1 Peter 2:23). We must continue to strive to love our neighbors as ourselves (Matthew 22:39).

We all know we shouldn't gossip. Yet our thirst for "news" (both hearing and telling) at times seems insatiable. Consequently, we devise ways of sharing it that salve our consciences. Will Rogers quipped, "The only time people dislike gossip is when you gossip about them."

SLANDER

Next of kin to gossip is slander. While gossip is often done in the context of idle, careless chatter, slander is the open, intentional sharing of damaging information. The Jews of the intertestamental period called the source of slander "the third tongue" because it is fatal to three sets of people: those who *speak* the slander, those who *listen* to it, and those *about* whom it is spoken.

Slander is pictured in both Hebrew and Greek in several definitive ways. A frequent Old Testament word for slander implies a somewhat neutral sense of *bad reports* in general. It is used when Joseph told his father of the wickedness of his brothers (Genesis 37:2) and when the ten spies brought back a negative report about the Promised Land (Numbers 13:32; 14:36–37). This same word is translated by the Hebrew lexicon as "to defame" or to strip one of his positive reputation.

Another Hebrew word for slander literally means "to blemish or to fault" (Psalm 50:20). It is interesting that the Old Testament word for *foot* is the root for the word translated both "spy" and "slander." The implication is that some people thrive so much on slander that they search for information and, as the lexicon says, "go about maliciously as slanderers" (2 Samuel 19:27).

In the New Testament, the word for slander is comprised of two words, one meaning "against" and the other meaning "to speak." So a slanderer is one who speaks against another (James 4:11; 1 Peter 2:1). Interestingly, the word for *devilish* or *diabolic* is translated as "slander" in the King James Version (1 Timothy 3:11) and "malicious talkers" in the New International Version. For example, a deacon's wife is not to engage in slanderous (literally *diabolic*), malicious speech.

Combining these various definitions, we discover that slander is characterized by bad reports that blemish or defame a person's reputation. Slander characterizes a wicked, godless heart (Psalm 50:16–23; Romans 1:28–30) and is a direct violation of God's Law (Leviticus 19:16).

Scripture couldn't be more clear in its denouncement of slander: "Do not speak against one another, brethren. He who speaks against a brother, or judges his brother, speaks against the law, and judges the law; but if you judge the law, you are not a doer of the law, but a judge of it. There is only one Lawgiver and Judge, the One who is able to save and to destroy; but who are you who judge your neighbor?" (James 4:11–12).

Slander disqualifies us for fellowship with God (Psalm 15:13). When we destroy with our tongues those whom God loves and wants to restore, we place ourselves in opposition to God and His purpose. Not only does slander alienate us spiritually, but it also brings God's "silencing" work into our lives (Psalm 101:5). If we refuse to keep our tongues from slander, then God, in His disciplining grace, will attempt to correct us (Proverbs 3:11–12).

Late one night I was listening to a radio preacher as he was scolding his congregation for hurting the testimony of Christ with their words. He said, "I can understand why a hungry man would steal to eat, but I can't understand why any Christian would ever speak like that! If I were the Lord, I'd give you throat cancer right now!" I was glad he *wasn't* the Lord, because I don't believe that's what God intends for us. But I do know that He has many creative ways to effect a silencing work in our lives.

If we slander someone, we run the risk of being branded as a slanderer for the rest of our lives, for bad reputations are hard to live down (Proverbs 25:9–10). Slander has a boomerang effect (30:10). It can evoke the anger of both its targets and those who hear it.

Slander surrounds itself with mistrust, doubt, exaggeration, and pride. David says that terror, conspiracy, and plotting are the destructive bedfellows of slander (Psalm 31:13). It is an unfitting companion for a believer who wants to grow spiritually and reflect God's glory.

MYTH COMMUNICATION

Gossip and slander are obviously serious violations of God's will. Why, then, are they so prevalent? Perhaps we have neutralized ourselves with "good" excuses. Several myths surround the social sport of telling tales. Recognizing these myths will help us to extricate this verbal cancer from our conversation.

The first myth is that gossip and slander are "women's" sins. Twice Scripture attributes these problems specifically to women (1 Timothy 3:11; 5:13), yet nowhere does the Bible promote the notion that men aren't equally guilty. The only difference is that men prefer to call gossip and slander by other names, such as "shooting the breeze," "shop talk," or better yet, "problem solving."

The second myth is that if information is true, it's OK to

tell it. But truth is not the only standard we need to consider. While truth is certainly one issue, so are confidentiality and potential harm. Scripture provides more complete standards for our speech: "Let us pursue the things which make for peace and the building up of one another" (Romans 14:19), and "Let no unwholesome word proceed from your mouth, but only such a word as is good for edification according to the need of the moment, that it will give grace to those who hear" (Ephesians 4:29).

The third myth is that sharing prayer concerns justifies an exchange of sensitive information. There's no telling how much gossip and slander have been preceded by the phrase, "this problem needs a lot of prayer." We Christians are good at participating in destructive communication even while considering ourselves holy.

Myth four relates to the unspoken desire for deeper relationships. Somehow we think we can enhance the depth of a relationship by sharing confidential or negative information about another person. In fact, some relationships would never exist if it weren't for a common enemy to talk about. But as we have learned, gossip and slander never deepen relationships; they ultimately separate them (Proverbs 16:28).

The fifth myth is that "the people I tell certainly won't tell anyone else." But if *you* promised secrecy to someone and are now willing to share information, what makes you think you can trust someone else to do any better?

WHAT TO DO WITH GOSSIP AND SLANDER

We must strip away these myths and ask, *What should we do with damaging information?* God's Word gives us four options. When you hear gossip or slander, you can:

1. Pray and leave the matter with God (1 Peter 5:7). Certain matters are beyond our human abilities to cope with or resolve. If we must talk to someone about them, it should be God.
2. Go directly to the subject of the gossip in a spirit of meekness and restoration (Matthew 18:15; Galatians

6:1). Unfortunately, the person who is being talked about is often the last one to hear the story. As one person said, "I was the talk of the town and didn't even know it." After hearing the individual's point of view, you may get a new perspective on the information.

3. Take the information to one who is in a place of authority to rectify the situation (Matthew 18:15–17; Romans 13:1–5).

4. Seek to protect the victim of the slander (Proverbs 10:12). After the Flood, one of Noah's sons found him in a drunken stupor in his tent. He "saw the nakedness of his father, and told his two brothers outside" (Genesis 9:22). But rather than keep the gossip chain going, the other two brothers attempted to protect their father's dignity. They took a blanket and walked backward into the tent to cover Noah without seeing his nakedness (v. 23). Afterward, Noah blessed his tactful sons and cursed the other one. A few seconds' thrill of spreading juicy gossip was not worth a lifetime of his father's displeasure.

We too will occasionally have the choice of revealing all we know about others or showing love by covering their shame. In the long run, the wiser choice is always to protect others as we are able. "Love covers all transgressions. . . . He who covers a transgression seeks love, but he who repeats a matter separates intimate friends" (Proverbs 10:12; 17:9).

A long-standing feud was brought to a sudden end by a Chinese farmer in 1991. His wife and his father refused to get along, and the twenty-four-year-old man was caught in the middle. After slander had bounced back and forth for a long time, in desperation to avoid taking sides, the farmer picked up a pair of scissors and cut off his tongue. I'm not recommending such drastic action, yet we might need to "swallow our tongues" to avoid getting involved in gossip and slander. It may even seem painful to miss opportunities to join others in their verbal bad habits. Yet, in such cases, silence is surely the better option.

If we don't eliminate gossip and slander from our conversations, we become like social cannibals who devour one another. "You were called to freedom, brethren; only do not turn your freedom into an opportunity for the flesh, but through love serve one another. For the whole Law is fulfilled in one word, in the statement, 'You shall love your neighbor as yourself.' But if you bite and devour one another, take care that you are not consumed by one another" (Galatians 5:13–15).

The choice is clear. We can chomp down on every bit of gossip that comes along and participate in all the backbiting that is involved in slander. Or we can cleanse our palate with love and practice the genuine freedom that is available only to God's people. Ask anyone who knows: the second option will leave a much better taste in your mouth.

On the surface, boasting may seem like an innocent pastime. After all, "If you've got it, flaunt it." Some of us have come to realize that if we don't praise ourselves, no one will.

These shallow excuses notwithstanding, boasting is social suicide. Even the basic rules of communication dictate that we talk about the interests of others and not of ourselves. By bringing attention to his own glory, a boaster aborts the very purpose of redemption, which is to bring glory to God (1 Corinthians 6:19–20). There are three pointed descriptions of those who boast.

The Inflated Zero

"Do nothing out of selfish ambition or vain conceit, but in humility consider others better than yourselves" (Philippians 2:3 NIV). The word for "vain conceit" comes from two Greek words meaning empty and glory. Vain conceit is the glorification of emptiness—the promotion of our "zeroness." God says that in our sinful natures there dwells nothing that is good (Romans 7:18). Even our finest efforts aside from Him have the value of "filthy rags" (Isaiah 64:6 NIV). Jesus said, "Apart from Me you can do nothing" (John 15:5). When I bring glory to myself, it is then the glory of my emptiness. We should remember that empty barrels make the most noise.

No matter how big my zero is, it's still a zero. When I boast of myself, it is nothing more than the enlargement of my emptiness. It is vain conceit. My life, my works, and all that I am take on meaning only in and through Christ. "I have been crucified with Christ; and it is no longer I who live, but Christ lives in me; and the life which I now live in the flesh I live by faith in the Son of God, who loved me and delivered Himself up for me" (Galatians 2:20). When something good is done in me, it is of Him and not of me.

A seminary classmate of mine was a bank teller in Dallas. Completing some paperwork at his window, he noticed our professor of Hebrew at the next teller's window. At the close of the transaction, the professor stepped away from the window and counted his money. Realizing that he had been given too much cash, he approached the window and told the teller.

She counted the money and said, "My, you're an honest man."

He carefully replied, "It's not that I'm an honest man; it's that Jesus Christ has changed my life."

He knew that all that was good in him was of Christ, and he tactfully gave God the credit. A boaster has no such perception.

The Wandering Quack

In the Old West, covered wagons would roll into town and, from the backs of the wagons, potions and elixirs were sold to remedy all ills. From consumption to gout, one bottle cured it all. Gullible people bought, and the wagon disappeared into the sunset. These early American medicine men claimed to deliver more than they could. The Bible would classify them as braggarts.

The word translated *boast* in James 4:16 literally means a "wandering quack." A braggart boasts about things he can't control and promises more than he can deliver. The context relates it to those who say, "Today or tomorrow we shall go to such and such a city, and spend a year there and engage in business and make a profit" (v. 13). But we do not have ultimate control over what we can or cannot do. God sovereignly guides our courses of life. "Instead, you ought to say, 'If the Lord wills, we will live and also do this or that'" (v. 15). This puts God in His proper role as the true governor of the affairs of our lives.

If any of us succeed, it is by God's careful and wise design. If we boast in our own abilities, then we speak as though there were no God. Such is the boaster's folly. "All such boasting is evil" (v. 16).

Embezzlers of God's Glory

One of the lowest forms of egomania is taking credit when it belongs to someone else. "Giving credit where credit is due" reflects a basic tenet of proper speech. It also reflects why God considers boasting such a serious offense.

The basic purpose of our existence is to reflect God's glory. God has designed His glory to be reflected through the universe, the children of Israel, the Word of God, Christ, humanity, and the believer. We glorify God by demonstrating who and what He is through our attitudes and activities. Paul told the believers in Corinth, "Know ye not that your body is the temple of the Holy Ghost which is in you, which ye have of God, and ye are not your own? For ye are bought with a price: therefore glorify God in your body" (1 Corinthians 6:19–20 KJV).

I've often wondered about God's denial of Moses' entrance into the Promised Land. Certainly there was more to it than just an angry striking of the rock. Psalm 106:33 says that Moses "spake unadvisedly with his lips" (KJV). In Numbers 20, we read that Moses said to the Israelites, "Shall we bring forth water for you out of this rock?" (v. 10). Moses had taken the honor that belonged to God. It was because he embezzled God's glory that he was not permitted into the Promised Land.

In a study of morality in America, *Psychology Today* found that 95 percent of those polled agreed that "accepting praise for another's work" was unethical (James Hassett, "But That Would Be Wrong," *Psychology Today,* November 1981, p. 34). If our relativistic culture is sensitive to this matter, we can imagine how God must view our accepting credit for His work in us.

For Herod, accepting the praise of men who acclaimed him as God meant instant death. "Immediately an angel of the Lord struck him because he did not give God the glory, and he was eaten by worms and died" (Acts 12:23).

Is it any wonder that when it came to the important process of salvation, God did all the work to make it possible? He knew if we helped save ourselves, we'd boast about it. That's why eternal life is "not a result of works, so that no one should boast" (Ephesians 2:9).

In each of these three pictures of boasting, God is denied His rightful place. In the inflation of our nothingness, God's work in us is ignored. When we boast of our abilities, we disregard God's divine oversight and control of our lives.

It is not surprising that when God's Word lists the characteristics of godless people, boasters often find their places in the list. In Romans 1, boasters are included in the godless company of slanderers, God-haters, the insolent, and the arrogant (Romans 1:30). Paul describes the godless in the last days by saying they will be "lovers of themselves, lovers of money, boastful, proud, abusive, disobedient to their parents, ungrateful, unholy" (2 Timothy 3:2 NIV).

"O Lord, the God who avenges, O God who avenges, shine forth. Rise up, O Judge of the earth; pay back to the proud what they deserve. How long will the wicked, O Lord, how long will the wicked be jubilant? They pour out arrogant words; all the evildoers are full of boasting" (Psalm 94:1–4 NIV).

If we must boast, the Bible instructs us to boast in God. "I will bless the Lord at all times; His praise shall continually be in my mouth. My soul shall make its boast in the Lord; the humble shall hear it and rejoice. O magnify the Lord with me, and let us exalt His name together" (Psalm 34:1–3). This boasting in the Lord is not only right, but it is also an encouragement to others. Conversely, when we boast about ourselves, we hurt those who are not as blessed as we might be.

In my first pastorate, God blessed the work beyond my expectations. I recall attending pastors' meetings where I would be asked how things were going. In my lack of sensitivity, I would recite the great things that were happening. It wasn't long until I realized that these words brought discouragement to the other pastors' hearts, especially those whose ministries were small, struggling, and often filled with division and hard feelings. I was communicating a boastful spirit even though I sometimes would sanctimoniously give God the credit as a ritualistic "P. S." When the Lord brought this to my attention, I found that I could have a ministry of encouragement to my fellow pastors by "boasting in the Lord." Comments like "The Lord has proven faithful" and "He's providing wisdom" put us on common ground. Turning the conversation then to *their* needs provided an opportunity for me to encourage them.

FLATTERY

The well-worn quip "Flattery will get you everywhere" is more truth than fiction. Few skills of the tongue are more manipulative, more ego-serving than flattery. This is the hypnotic power of the tongue to seduce and to conquer.

Flattery is the act of placing someone in debt to us by verbally commending some action, virtue, or involvement in his life. The commendation may or may not be true. Flattery differs from genuine praise or compliment because of its motive —it is a compliment shared to manipulate another for personal gain.

There are at least four manipulative abilities within the scope of a flatterer's tongue. *Attention* is one of the payoffs for flattery. If I tell you what a great job you did in the Sunday school discussion, you will pay attention to me. You will smile, look at me, and thank me. Some of us are so starved for that kind of attention that we use undue adulation to get it.

Sometimes flattery is used to *solicit compliments*. Few of us would be so forward as to ask someone to compliment our new clothes. But we might flatter other people about *their* attractive clothes and hope that they return the compliment. Our flattery puts others in debt to our positive comments about them.

The flatterer uses the power of his words to seduce. Immoral, unethical, cruel, and damaging partnerships have often been sealed in a flatterer's parlor. Statements such as "You're a beautiful woman. I just love the way you wear your hair," "I know you're smart enough to know a good deal when you see one," and "I wish my husband were as kind and sensitive as you are" are all traps set in the web of a flatterer's tongue. As Samuel Johnson said, "Men are like stone jugs— you may lug them where you like by their ears."

The flatterer also uses his words to *gain favor*. All of us like to be esteemed and liked by others. True favor comes by *earning* another's respect. Unfortunately, some of us think we can worm our way into other people's favor by flattering them. There are no shortcuts to real respect and solid relationships. In the long run, ingratiating speech only damages and spoils the potential of respect and high regard.

The sin of flattery is linked with godlessness, faithlessness, oppression, pride, wickedness, and all that is vile. "Help, Lord, for the godly man ceases to be, for the faithful disappear from among the sons of men. They speak falsehood to one another; with flattering lips and with a double heart they speak. May the Lord cut off all flattering lips, the tongue that speaks great things; who have said, 'With our tongue we will prevail; our lips are our own; who is lord over us?'" (Psalm 12:1–4).

In Psalm 5:9, the word translated *flatter* literally means to "make their tongue smooth." Flatterers employ slick speech. The New International Version translates the word *deceit*. Flattery is a smooth and subtle form of deceit. This makes it difficult to discern. The smooth deceit is doubly dangerous because most of us enjoy the flattery.

Psalm 5:9 also states that a flatterer's words cannot be trusted. "There is nothing reliable in what they say." Lastly, verse 9 says that flatterers' throats are like open graves.

Flattery is a reflection of a destructive spirit. When we seek to control or use others for our benefit, we begin to destroy them. A flatterer destroys the object of his flattery by placing the potential of pride and the snare of seduction in his path.

The psalmist recognized this danger in verse 8: "O Lord, lead me in Your righteousness because of my foes; make Your way straight before me." The word *foes* in this verse actually means "those who lie in wait for me." We should heed God's warning: "A man who flatters his neighbor is spreading a net for his steps" (Proverbs 29:5).

This, of course, does not mean that we should never genuinely compliment, encourage, or praise someone who deserves or needs a positive word. The key is the motivation. Why am I complimenting this person? If it truly is an act of love, encouragement, and support with no thought of personal gain, then it is a compliment, not flattery.

Compliments that give glory to God shield others from the traps of pride and seduction. Comments such as "I'm thankful the Lord has given you such a spirit of encouragement," "God has been good to give me a husband like you," or "The Lord has given you a special ability to minister to me through song" go a long way to take flattery out of our compliments.

EXAGGERATION

Someone once said, "I don't exaggerate—I just stretch the truth." Exaggeration is nothing more than lying about details to make information more sensational, interesting, or manipulative. From fishermen to politicians, no one is exempt from this ego-serving tendency of the tongue.

This form of lying is prevalent. Some of us exaggerate to catch people's attention. Have you ever been telling a story when you suddenly realized that you were losing your audience's interest? Almost subconsciously, we add a little zip to the drama. What was only a broken toe at first becomes fatal cancer of the foot after several tellings. We all add a little of our own pizzazz until we have made a mountain out of a molehill.

Have you ever exaggerated to manipulate someone into doing what you wanted them to do? "I'll knock your head off if you don't come here" is the manipulative exaggeration of an angry parent. In fact, anger often vents itself in exaggerated expressions to intimidate or humble those we are angry with. I get a chuckle out of King Nebuchadnezzar who, in his great anger against Shadrach, Meshach, and Abednego, commanded that the furnace be turned up seven times hotter (Daniel 3:19). The fire would have been sufficient just the way it was, but in his anger Nebuchadnezzar had an exaggerated response.

Sometimes we exaggerate to feel better about ourselves and to help others feel better about us as well. The fisherman whose largemouth bass was *just* three pounds ends up telling people that it was *at least* three pounds. The businessman who makes $50,000 a year tells his friend that he's making "something under $100,000 a year." Salesmen face a special temptation in this area. How easy it is to exaggerate the claims of a product to close a sale.

I worked for a carpenter one summer. Occasionally, I would cut a board too short, and he would say, "Get the wood stretcher." His joke, of course, was that wood doesn't stretch. But this isn't a joke: The truth doesn't stretch either. Some of us want to make Silly Putty of the truth by stretching it to our own fancy. The problem is that stretching the truth destroys it.

Exaggeration erodes trust and credibility, two building blocks of successful relationships. It is a violation of God's will for us. Yielding our egos to be used to serve God and others instead of our own interests will produce words that help and heal. Then with the psalmist we can say, "Let the words of my mouth and the meditation of my heart be acceptable in Your sight, O Lord, my rock and my Redeemer" (Psalm 19:14).

5

CROSS WORDS

Murmuring and Contentious Words

I recall hanging wallpaper in our kitchen one evening.
Everything was ready—the tarp, the tools, and the water
trough, which was filled and in place on the floor. I was
inspecting the wall to be papered when I heard a sound
behind me that I shouldn't have—the *swoosh* of flowing
water. I turned to look, and my worst fears were realized.
There stood my youngest son, Matthew, one foot in the
trough, one foot in spilled water, and two apprehensive eyes
glued on me. I shook my head and said with obvious irritation, "You klutz."

Immediately, Matthew began to cry. Two words from me
were all it took to pierce his young spirit, puncturing his
sense of worth and value. The spilled water was no longer
important; the issue was now our relationship. It took hugs
and reassuring words to convince him that Daddy's words
and attitude had been wrong and that I still thought he was
the greatest seven-year-old in the whole world.

Our tongues are like Swiss Army knives in their versatility
for expressing anger. We can show displeasure with complaining, screaming, subtle barbs, nagging, criticism, and
angry words. We can verbally cut and destroy others in
numerous ways. Proverbs says this about the piercing tenden-
cies of the tongue: "There is one who speaks rashly like the
thrusts of a sword, but the tongue of the wise brings healing"

(12:18). And the psalmist describes the tongue as a "sharp sword" and a "serpent" (Psalm 57:4; 140:3).

We use cross words for a number of different reasons. Here is a brief list of the most common reasons for our verbal outbursts:

- *Anger.* Anger is like an inner explosion searching for an outlet. A common escape valve is the tongue. Angry people are frequently quarrels looking for a place to happen.

- *Irritation.* Sharp words often result from irritation that is produced when people interrupt or interfere with our well-ordered lives.

- *Disappointment.* If our disappointment in a person or a situation is strong enough, our words will reflect it. Unrealized expectations are painful, and our disappointment shows up in our speech.

- *Impatience.* Impetuous spirits have a tendency to let loose with verbal outbursts before giving the situation appropriate thought.

- *Stress.* People in frequent emotional "overload" tend to have shorter verbal fuses than those who live in an organized, relaxed environment.

- *Insecurity.* Insecure people may resort to sharp, intimidating, critical words in order to project a sense of strength and security. Unfortunately, their cross words only weaken relationships and compound insecurity.

- *Guilt.* When guilty people are confronted, they often respond sharply. Retorts such as "Who do you think you are?" or "I suppose you think you're perfect!" are the barbed defense mechanisms spoken by a person with a guilty conscience.

Scripture indicates that these root issues surface in our speech in two general ways. One is the verbal sin of *murmuring.* The other is called a *contentious tongue.*

MURMURING

Talking with a Christian doctor about his family, I learned that all of his children were grown, happily committed to Christ, and serving in their local churches. The doctor was obviously grateful and relieved that his children had grown in the faith. As a father of three, I was intensely interested in knowing what he thought was the secret to the spiritual maturity of his children.

He told me, "My wife and I covenanted that our children would never hear us complain or criticize the church, church leaders, or another brother or sister in Christ."

In essence, he had made a commitment not to murmur.

Murmuring is a form of complaining that harbors a negative attitude toward a situation or the people involved. It runs the continuum from griping about the slow driver in front of you to murmuring against the Lord for things He has permitted to come into your life. The common factor in all murmuring is a critical spirit. This kind of grumbling carries the potential for great damage and is a direct violation of God's will.

My doctor friend wisely realized that complaining about God's work or God's people was a direct reflection on the value of God and His plan. What children would want to commit their lives to a church that is the constant object of their parents' complaints? Wise parents teach and model principles of love and prayerful intercession in regard to imperfections around them. Hearing murmuring about the family of God only gives a young child excuses for future rebellion.

Nowhere in Scripture is murmuring more graphically depicted than in the case of the Israelites on their way to the Promised Land. When they arrive on the outskirts, twelve spies were sent to "case out" the territory. Ten spies returned with a negative report about what they had seen: "We are not able to go up against the people, for they are too strong for us. . . . The land through which we have gone, in spying it out, is a land that devours its inhabitants; and all the people whom we saw in it are men of great size. . . . We became like

grasshoppers in our own sight, and so we were in their sight"
(Numbers 13:31–33). Joshua and Caleb, the other two spies,
had seen the same things. However, they advised moving forward because they had faith that God was able to deliver them.

Several aspects of this story are instructive:

1. *Murmuring ignores God's potential.* The report of the ten
   spies reflected a godless perspective. God had opened
   the sea to save them, the heavens to feed them, and the
   rocks to provide water for them. He had defeated
   mighty armies throughout their wilderness trek. He
   had freed them from perhaps the most powerful
   nation on the planet. Certainly He could deal with any
   problems the new land might present.

2. *Murmuring is born in the context of bad reports.* Sins of the
   tongue that spread negative reports (beguilement,
   gossip, slander, false witness) create an environment in
   which murmuring can thrive. Some people are always
   eager to hear negative things so they can have something to complain about.

3. *A murmuring spirit is quick to jump to the wrong conclusion.*
   The grumbling Israelites blamed God for their situation and even started planning to return to Egypt
   (14:3)! Actually, God was as much in control as He had
   ever been. But once godless grumbling begins to
   spread, wrong conclusions are easily reached. Murmuring and beguilement go hand in hand.

4. *Bad judgments are spawned in the atmosphere of murmuring.*
   The murmuring Israelites decided it would have been
   better to have died in Egypt. In their haste to return,
   they even attempted to stone the ones urging them to
   stop grumbling and trust in the Lord (14:10). Murmuring distorts good judgment.

5. *Murmuring leads to self-pity.* "Would that we had died in
   the land of Egypt! Or would that we had died in this
   wilderness!" (v. 2). Murmurers often feel sorry for
   themselves and focus on how they have been mistreated, misused, and let down.

6. *Murmuring thrives in an atmosphere of fear.* Twice Joshua and Caleb exhorted the people not to be afraid (v. 9). But the Israelites' fear of the unknown fanned the sparks of grumbling in their midst. They were in a situation beyond their control, and they felt threatened and insecure. Their faith disappeared as their fear increased.

7. *Murmuring left unchecked usually breeds rebellion.* Joshua and Caleb urged the murmuring Israelites not to "rebel against the Lord" (v. 9). But rather than listen to reason, the Israelites were ready to elect new leaders who would oversee their rebellious plans.

8. *The end result of a murmuring spirit is a general atmosphere of dissatisfaction.* Criticism and complaining lead to discontent. By the end of this episode, Israel was dissatisfied with their God-given lot in life. "Majority reports" are not always trustworthy. Just because a lot of people are murmuring doesn't necessarily mean they are right. But we tend to wear fear and insecurity close to the surface, so murmuring has no trouble attracting a crowd.

God's judgment on the Israelites was swift and final. Their murmuring had verbally defamed His presence, power, wisdom, and glory. They would not see the Promised Land, and they would be granted their misguided wish to die in the wilderness.

The New Testament describes other situations that involved murmuring. The Pharisees murmured because of ignorance and lack of information (John 6:41–43). When the early church didn't adequately meet the needs of Greek widows, the Grecians murmured in the congregation (Acts 6:1). After Paul reminds us that "it is God who is at work in you, both to will and to work for His good pleasure" (Philippians 2:13), he then challenges us to, "Do all things without grumbling or disputing" (2:14). The presence of God and His power in us is a sufficient resource to help us cope with problems without murmuring.

Murmuring is always a godless pastime. It's a habit that thwarts our potential in God. It refuses to believe that God can conquer any problem or condition. And it refuses to recognize that God may use negative circumstances to accomplish His best in our lives and demonstrate His glory.

Is it ever right to express dissatisfaction? Certainly, as long as our attitudes remain grounded in the belief that God is in control and can intervene or not as He so desires. Three steps help to keep our complaints constructive:

1. *Pray.* The psalmist often complained to God about his problems. However, he never lost confidence in God's faithfulness, power, and love. In praying we should commit our problems to God's care and willingly wait for Him to direct us to His solution.

2. *Take your complaints to someone with the authority to rectify the situation.* Sharing problems with those who are not a part of the solution only stimulates murmuring and makes resolution more difficult. Assure the person in authority of your loyalty and desire to help. Open your mind to his or her perspective.

3. *Direct others to sources of help.* When people come to you with problems, encourage them to go to someone in authority before discussing their situations with you any further. While it never hurts to be a good listener, many times others are looking for allies in their murmuring. Don't get caught in the middle of a conflict if you have no opportunity to bring the disagreement to an end.

THE CONTENTIOUS TONGUE

An old farm couple who had experienced a rocky marriage were riding in their wagon one evening. As the two horses pulled them along in the moonlight, something of the early romance rekindled in the heart of the wife. She snuggled up to her husband, took his arm, and remarked about how nicely the horses worked together, separated only by the tongue of the wagon. The husband, after a second of thought, drawled, "We could probably get along better too if we had only one tongue between us."

Contentious tongues create strife, resentment, and division in any relationship. Biblical references to a contentious tongue stem mostly from a few Hebrew words that mean "to have a cause." Though many causes are good and constructive, we often refer to "having a cause" in the context of a negative, vengeful spirit. It is in these cases that the words are translated *contention, strife, quarreling,* and *debating.*

God's Word provides a list of causes for a contentious tongue. *Hatred* (Proverbs 10:12) and a *hot temper* (15:18) are obvious roots. *Anger* is added to the list with a colorful description from Proverbs 30:33: "For the churning of milk produces butter, and pressing the nose brings forth blood; so the churning of anger produces strife." *Arrogance* (resulting in greed) is yet another source (28:25). People intent on personal gain stir up dissension. Children who refuse to share their toys create a spirit of contention with their peers, to say nothing of the children who grab the toys of others for themselves. Adults simply translate toys into dollars and possessions. A contentious tongue is often the inevitable by-product of a greedy heart.

Contention may also be bred by *close quarters and an insufficient supply of provisions.* Genesis 13 describes a conflict between the herdsmen of Abraham and the herdsmen of Lot because the land could not support both herds. Though most of us don't fight over pastureland, we may be quick to put contentious tongues to work over offices with insufficient supplies, homes with insufficient room, and relationships with too much competition.

A *desire for position and prestige* is another cause of contentious words. This tendency toward "big shotitis" was present even among Jesus' disciples. After three years of sitting under Christ's ministry, they were still contending with each other over who would be the greatest in the kingdom (Luke 22:24). In fact, that was the subject of the conversation in the Upper Room the night before Christ went to the Cross. On another occasion, the mother of James and John asked that her sons would have the highest positions of prestige in the coming kingdom. When the other ten heard about it, they were indignant (Matthew 20:20–28).

It should come as no surprise that *an addiction to alcohol or other drugs* results in a life of strife. Scripture lists many symptoms of "those who linger long over wine" (Proverbs 23:29–30). Innumerable homes and relationships deteriorate into contentiousness because of addictions.

One common form of verbal contention is nagging. While I know of men who nag with the best of them, it seems that women have more of a reputation in regard to this problem. And apparently the problem goes back a long way. The author of Proverbs states that it is preferable to live "in a corner of a roof" or "in a desert land" than to endure a "contentious and vexing" woman (Proverbs 21:9, 19).

We tend to downplay the seriousness of nagging, but I recall a murder trial in the Chicago area several years ago where a man testified that he killed his wife because she nagged him about his drinking. During a quarrel, she became angry and threw a couple of hairbrushes at him. In retaliation, he picked up a .45 caliber handgun and shot her dead. Obviously, there were deeper problems between this couple, but the incident was ignited by nagging. Beware!

In cases like this, it becomes clear that many wives find themselves with responsibilities over which they have limited control. A wife, by the nature of her role, is especially vulnerable to hurts and disappointments. She would like her husband to communicate with her and to participate (at least mentally) in her life and interests. She wants him to share her concern for the children's welfare and the spiritual climate of the home. Yet many husbands fall far short of these hopes and expectations. Consequently, nagging may become a wife's attempt to get the husband's attention. Fortunately, Scripture does provide other ways to cope with these pressures. But for the wife or mother who has not discovered God's better way, nagging can be simply a matter of survival.

The most serious result of a contentious tongue is the division and discord it creates. Unity is extremely important to God and should be to His people as well (John 17:11). Yet a quarreling, bickering, contentious tongue divides rather than unifies. When contentious words cause divisions in the church or at home, we destroy not only the joy of oneness but also the reflection of God in our midst. In fact, the infamous list of seven things that are an abomination to the Lord (Proverbs 6:16–19) ends emphatically with anyone "who spreads strife among brothers."

Paul scolded the Corinthians for being contentious with each other (1 Corinthians 3:3). Then he defined the church as the body of Christ, intended to work as a single unit in cooperative harmony (12:12–31). Have you ever seen a body cut into several parts functioning well? Division among the brethren destroys the reflection of God through us.

I recall watching a butcher prepare a chicken. His sharp cleaver chopped away with calculated, well-timed strokes until the bird lay in a dozen pieces. Contentious words are like that meat cleaver. They divide something that was intended to be together.

On the home front, my relationship with my spouse is God's living illustration of Christ and the church. Christ never divides Himself from His bride, the church. His unconditional love and acceptance are unifying factors. His words to the church promote healing and growth. If contentious words divide our spirits at home, we destroy the God-intended picture of Christ and His church.

The phrase "divide and conquer" has spiritual validity. Division among God's people gives Satan a tremendous advantage in squelching our usefulness, joy, and peace. The destructive influence of murmuring, contentious words must be exchanged for words that produce confidence in Christ and encouragement to His people. As Paul says, "Let no unwholesome word proceed from your mouth, but only such a word as is good for edification according to the need of the moment, that it will give grace to those who hear" (Ephesians 4:29).

6

EXPLETIVES DELETED

Using God's Name in Vain and Sensuous Speech

When the transcripts of the Watergate tapes came to light, a new phrase was introduced to the American public: "Expletives deleted." President Nixon and some of his associates used language that the government and the media didn't want to repeat verbatim. "Expletives deleted" soon became a common term as a reference to less-than-uplifting speech.

It's a sad reflection on our culture, but many of those expletives are no longer as offensive as they once were. Even prime-time television programs today use words and phrases that once were forbidden by network censors. Like many standards of society, the rules of speech are not absolute, but relative.

Some whose job it is to manage and motivate people claim that expletives communicate the seriousness of a matter. To them, an appropriate expletive shows that you mean business. And just recently a judge ruled that vulgar and profane speech in the workplace is not only allowable but even serves to bring people closer together in a sense of camaraderie. While society seems to be deleting fewer and fewer expletives, Christians need to remember that God's Word establishes absolute parameters for our speech.

USING GOD'S NAME IN VAIN

The clear rule for using God's name in vain is "Thou shalt not" (Exodus 20:7, KJV). Of all the Ten Commandments, this one includes a particularly stern emphasis. God not only prohibits the misuse of His name, but He also warns of coming punishment for those who disobey.

Taking God's name "in vain" literally means to use it for something that is "waste and in disorder; hence that which is empty, vain . . . for which there is no occasion" (Keil and Deilitzsh, *The Pentateuch,* vol. 2 of *Commentaries on the Old Testament,* Eerdmans, p. 118). Essentially, to take God's name in vain means to use it as though it has no worth or value.

Perhaps that's the root of our problem—we don't appreciate the real value of God's name. Too often we interpret God from our limited point of view instead of conforming our thoughts to who God says He is. Our shortsighted perceptions of God insult Him by attempting to bring Him down to our level. The result is distorted thinking and idolatry.

In our culture, names most often are merely cosmetic. When a child is born, a name is frequently chosen because it sounds pleasant. For most of us, names have no intrinsic value. But God's name is different because it has value and worth. The significance of God's name must be grasped in two dimensions: (1) its significance to God, and (2) its experiential significance to us.

First, God's name has great significance to Him because it is a revelation of His glory. His name communicates His character. It is intrinsically tied to His being.

When God spoke to Moses at the burning bush, Moses wanted to know what to tell the Israelites if they were to ask God's name. God's reply is enlightening:

> God said to Moses, "I AM WHO I AM"; and He said, "Thus you shall say to the sons of Israel, 'I AM has sent me to you.'" God, furthermore, said to Moses, "Thus you shall say to the sons of Israel, 'The Lord, the God of your fathers, the God of Abraham, the God of Isaac, and the God of Jacob, has sent me to you.' This is My name forever, and this is My memorial-name to all generations." (Exodus 3:14–15)

God's name revealed that He was the eternally self-existent One, personally identified with Israel through the patriarchs. Throughout the Old Testament, God's names reveal detailed aspects of His glory. Even the word *name,* used in reference to God, became an all-inclusive statement for the revelation of all that God is.

The psalmist said, "I will tell of Your name to my brethren" (Psalm 22:22). In other words, "I will speak about all that You are." When Isaiah warned that the "name of the Lord" was coming, he meant that God was coming in all of His justice, wrath, and holiness (Isaiah 30:27). The Old Testament proclaims that God's name will endure forever (Psalm 72:17) and that "The name of the Lord is a strong tower; the righteous runs into it and is safe" (Proverbs 18:10). An awareness of these realities helps us develop a true sense of the dignity, worth, and value that belong to God's name.

The names for Jesus are also revelatory of His character, worth, and work. The name *Christ* is the title of His Messiahship, communicating that He is the promised King and reflecting the integrity of God in keeping His promise to Israel. *Immanuel* means "God with us" (Matthew 1:23). The name *Jesus* was especially prescribed by the angel because it is the word for "Savior." As the angel promised, "He will save His people from their sins" (v. 21).

The name of Jesus carries power over evil spirits (Matthew 7:22) and power in prayer (John 14:13–14). It is the authority by which the Holy Spirit comes (v. 26) as well as for salvation (Romans 10:13) and baptism (Matthew 28:19–20).

The name of Jesus is important to God the Father. Paul writes, "God highly exalted Him, and bestowed on Him the name which is above every name, so that at the name of Jesus every knee should bow . . . and that every tongue will confess that Jesus Christ is Lord, to the glory of God the Father" (Philippians 2:9–11). God guarantees that everyone will bow in response to Jesus' name in submission to all Christ claims to be. Even those who make an expletive of His name will one day exalt Him.

Likewise, the Father's name is important to Christ. When Jesus taught the disciples to pray, He began with, "Our Father who is in heaven, hallowed be Your name" (Matthew 6:9). The word *hallowed* literally means sacred, set apart, holy. This petition at the opening of the Lord's Prayer acknowledges that the Father's name is to be honored and revered. The sacredness of the Father's name was a priority concern of the Savior.

Old Testament Jews gave so much reverence to the name of Jehovah that they took away its vowels when they wrote it. When the name was symbolized rather than spoken, it could not be misspoken. Tradition says that at one point in their history, the Jews even refused to use God's name in a conversation with a non-Jew.

We are to regard God's name with appropriate respect today as well. Scripture provides numerous instructions for us, indicating that God's name is important to Him. We are to:

- Love God's name (Psalm 5:11).
- Wait on God's name (Psalm 52:9).
- Bless and praise God's name (Psalm 145:1–2).
- Walk in the name of the Lord (Micah 4:5).
- Esteem God's name (Malachi 3:16).
- Fear God's name (Malachi 4:2).

Theologically speaking, God's names are not adjectives—they are nouns. His names are more than descriptive; they are substantive.

Taking God's name in vain indicates a cooling in our religious temperature. When we use one of His names in an empty, negative context, it reveals a lowered estimation of His worth. Degrading God's name is the ultimate statement of a wicked and proud heart.

Since God's name is of great significance to Him, it should be just as significant to us. Names gain value and worth by experience. For example, my wife may prefer Amy as the name for a baby girl, but I may remember an Amy who always refused to go out with me on dates. I might hope to name her Samantha, but perhaps Samantha was the name of a mean girl on my wife's block. If so, our child isn't likely to be named either Amy or Samantha. My wife and I would work to choose a name we both valued.

When I was in high school, the greatest insult you could hurl at another guy was to use his mother's name in some crude context. "Mother" meant something special; it represented worth and value. It was a violation of both heart and mind to hear it used wrongly.

The names of those we love are precious to us. It upsets us to hear others demean them. Yet perhaps we aren't as quick to take offense when God's name is misused. Believers should be especially careful not to use God's name in callous, casual, or flippant ways. Expressions such as "Oh, God," "God," and "My Lord" are often used as verbal exclamation points. Jokes that make light of His value and holiness are woven into the social fare of some Christian gatherings. Even expressions such as "Praise the Lord" are thrown around with such frequency that they become essentially meaningless.

As we mature spiritually, God should become more precious to us. As we experience the depth of His saving work, the name *Jesus* (Savior) becomes more endearing. As we realize the joy of submitting to His sovereign authority, the title *Lord* takes on special meaning. An increasing awareness of all that God is elevates His names in our hearts. We honor and revere them with our tongues.

SENSUOUS SPEECH

Expressions of immoral, sensual speech are not compatible with our newness in Christ. Words, phrases, stories, jokes, and tales that deal with immorality are clearly renounced in Scripture.

> But immorality or any impurity or greed must not even be named among you, as is proper among saints; and there must

be no filthiness and silly talk, or coarse jesting, which are not fitting, but rather giving of thanks. For this you know with certainty, that no immoral or impure person or covetous man, who is an idolater, has an inheritance in the kingdom of Christ and God. Let no one deceive you with empty words, for because of these things the wrath of God comes upon the sons of disobedience. Therefore do not be partakers with them; for you were formerly darkness, but now you are light in the Lord; walk as children of Light (for the fruit of the Light consists in all goodness and righteousness and truth), trying to learn what is pleasing to the Lord. Do not participate in the unfruitful deeds of darkness, but instead even expose them; for it is disgraceful even to speak of the things which are done by them in secret. (Ephesians 5:3–12)

Exposure to immoral speech comes from within through the nature of our flesh and from without due to the tremendous amount of corrupt input from our culture. We can feed our lusts twenty-four hours a day if we wish. Any number of ungodly influences are available to us—and not all of them seem "bad" or threatening. Even if we avoid obvious threats such as soft and hard pornography, we may let down our guard as we go to movies, rent videos, watch prime-time television (not to mention some cable channels), view our favorite soap operas, surf the Internet, and listen to music (not just rock 'n' roll, but country, blues, and so on). Harmful input is everywhere, both in overt and subtle ways. Even advertising is frequently based on sexual innuendos, if not outright seduction. With all of this input, it's difficult not to absorb some of the ungodly influences and recycle them as verbal output.

As Christians, our sensitivities have been dulled. What would have raised red flags just a few years ago now raises smiles and rapt attention with perhaps only a little twinge of conscience. Marginal expressions, questionable jokes, and phrases with double meanings are tolerated and often enjoyed. This, unfortunately, can lead to a greater openness to other sins. At the very least, it takes up a lot of our time that could be devoted to higher pursuits.

For example, I spoke at a deacons' retreat held by a solid,

biblically based church. I was looking forward to getting to know some of the men better, but I noticed many of them making a quick exodus from the dinner table Friday night. I discovered they were eager to get back to their rooms so they wouldn't miss the next episode of a popular television program that was noted for the adultery, unfaithfulness, greed, and violence of its characters.

To me, the mind-set of these Christian men was symptomatic. It said something about our insensitivity to moral impurity. Perhaps we have deceived ourselves into thinking we can be observers of these innumerable influences without having them affect our own speech and lifestyles.

GUIDELINES FOR PURE SPEECH

God draws a clear, immovable line in the sand of the moral desert of our day. The Ephesians also lived in an immoral culture, and Paul told them that immorality must not even be mentioned among believers (5:3). Paul lists filthiness, silly talk, and coarse jesting as things to be avoided (v. 4).

Filthiness, or obscenity, literally means anything that is opposed to purity or morality. Its antonym in the Greek means that which is good, moral, or beautiful. Words, expressions, stories, and conversations that oppose God's standards of purity and morality are out of bounds. Our newness in Christ demands clean, wholesome words.

Silly, or foolish, *talk* is described by one Greek scholar as language offensive to Christian decency. This would certainly include words that are vulgar and indecent in their connotations. Speech from a foolish heart is godless. Since God is pleased with modesty (1 Timothy 2:9), talk that condones immodesty is foolish. Since God is concerned about loyalty in marriage, conversations that make light of marital fidelity are foolish as well.

Coarse jesting, or joking, is the translation of a Greek word that literally means "that which turns easily." It is the lighthearted, sinful speech filled with double meanings—jokes, puns, and plays on words. Advertising, television dramas, and general conversation abound with coarse humor. It is so ingrained in us that it takes diligence to avoid getting our own tongues involved.

Ephesians 5 contains two appeals for morality in speech. The first is a reminder of our holy standard before God (Ephesians 5:1–3). The second appeal is to practice simple decency. Crude talk is "not fitting" for the Christian (v. 4). The same passage includes a number of warnings concerning sensual speech.

WARNINGS ABOUT SENSUAL SPEECH

First, we are warned to beware of those who would deceive us with empty words (Ephesians 5:6). This verse infers that deceit contradicts God's standards for behavior and speech, and it reminds us that God's wrath comes upon those who disobey His standards. Some people try to deceive others into thinking that those who adhere to God's moral standards are legalists. They cleverly appeal to our pride, challenging us to be "up-to-date," "open-minded," or able to deal with sinful input. God's Word says, "Do not be deceived, God is not mocked; for whatever a man sows, this he will also reap" (Galatians 6:7).

Second, we are warned against forming partnerships with moral decadence (Ephesians 5:7). Many people in our society don't think twice before delving into verbal, visual, and economic partnerships that are far from pure. Believers must learn to be a positive influence on the world without falling into sinful partnerships along the way (James 4:4).

Third, we must remember that we are children of the light (Ephesians 5:8). We are no longer a part of the darkness. Whenever we revert to our old patterns and involve ourselves in sin, we break our fellowship with God and violate His will for us (1 John 1:5–7; 2 Corinthians 6:14–7:1).

Whenever sensuous speech affects believers, the harmful results are numerous:

- It neutralizes our sensitivity to moral purity.
- It contributes to a widespread sensual mind-set.

- It reflects a lack of self-control.
- It increases our vulnerability to sexual sin.
- It robs God of His glory in our speech.

Paul provides two suggestions for transforming our sensuous speech patterns. First, we should speak words that are "good for edification according to the need of the moment, so that it will give grace to those who hear" (Ephesians 4:29). Sensuous speech obviously hinders. Instead of building up others, it weakens them. A commitment to words that build and benefit will eliminate sensuous speech.

We are also to enjoy the pleasure of sharing grateful words with each other (5:4). Immoral talk reflects immorality, which breeds discontent. By verbally and visually dwelling on our lusts, we develop an ungratefulness for what we presently have sexually. Such discontent leads some people on an insatiable journey through a series of sexual fantasies and experiments—always searching for, yet never finding, a fulfilling experience.

On the other hand, purity keeps our minds and lives uncluttered, free to know, experience, and proclaim God's greatness. Helpful, constructive, beneficial words—words that reflect the joy of thanksgiving and praise—are spoken from hearts that have been truly transformed.

Tongues that honor God's name and reflect purity are of value to God and others. As our words involve us in people's lives, may others note that the expletives have been deleted and replaced with something far better—a verbal reflection of the joy, contentment, and love for life that only God can bring.

7

HEART TALK

Your Tongue Reflects Your Spirit

As a boy, one of my responsibilities was to dig the dandelions out of our lawn. It didn't seem like such a bad job at first, but then my dad would always say, "Be sure to get the root." As long as the roots remained, the dandelions would keep growing back.

Dandelions have something in common with our tongues —they both have roots. If we try to resolve sinful speech patterns from the neck up, we soon find that the problems keep coming back. That's because our speech problems are really heart problems. Our tongues are the servants of our spirits. My words simply reveal what's on my heart.

Before we were married, my wife and I would often double-date with friends. On one such occasion we were driving home from a basketball game when Martie and I heard soft singing coming from the backseat. My friend was the star All-American pitcher for our college baseball team, and his date was one of the prettiest girls on campus. Yet this macho athlete was actually serenading his fiancée. Though it wasn't the usual approach to courtship, he had a "heart condition" that needed to be expressed.

All talk is really heart talk. Granted, some people's spoken thoughts never seem to reach down to the heart (or up to the brain, for that matter). But even empty flattery, thoughtless comments, automatic responses, and mindless greetings are reflections of an insincere heart.

Christ recognized that all talk is heart talk. He said:

> Either make the tree good and its fruit good, or make the tree bad, and its fruit bad; for the tree is known by its fruit. You brood of vipers, how can you, being evil, speak what is good? For the mouth speaks out of that which fills the heart. The good man brings out of his good treasure what is good; and the evil man brings out of his evil treasure what is evil. But I tell you that every careless word that people speak, they shall give an accounting for it in the day of judgment. For by your words you will be justified, and by your words you will be condemned. (Matthew 12:33–37)

Jesus' comments were in response to the Pharisees, who were downplaying His miracles by saying, "This man casts out demons only by Beelzebul the ruler of the demons" (v. 24). Christ responded by pointing out that what they said was a reflection of their wicked hearts.

In fact, our words are such an accurate reflection of our spiritual condition that Christ concludes this section by saying that our words will be the basis for His judgment. We will be held accountable for our words, not because God is a "nit-picker," but because our words affirm our true inner condition.

Paul reflects on heart talk when he writes:

> There is none righteous, not even one; there is none who understands, there is none who seeks for God; all have turned aside, together they have become useless; there is none who does good, there is not even one. Their throat is an open grave, with their tongues they keep deceiving, the poison of asps is under their lips; whose mouth is full of cursing and bitterness; their feet are swift to shed blood, destruction and misery are in their paths, and the path of peace they have not known. There is no fear of God before their eyes. (Romans 3:10–18)

Notice that after a general description of the Romans' spiritual disability, Paul specifically details the tongue as the initial manifestation of their inner worthlessness. I am struck by the emphasis on the tongue in this passage. Of all the ways by which we ventilate inner wickedness, the tongue receives priority attention.

A sinful heart produces sinful speech. The picture here is vivid: throats are portrayed as open graves. Open graves vent the smell of death. Our throats, tongues, and lips are all part of the ventilation of our inner spiritual condition.

My friends in medicine tell me that certain sicknesses produce terrible breath odors. So it is with sin. It is vented through the mouth, disseminated by the tongue, and its deadly potential waits in the lips.

I remember one day at kindergarten when I spouted off to my teacher. I can't recall what stimulated the upheaval, but eventually I told my teacher to shut up. Then I stood, left the room, and started walking home. But when I got within sight of my house and noticed my mother working in the backyard, I stopped dead in my tracks. What would I tell her?

My options seemed clear—face my mother, face the teacher, or walk alone into the big cruel world. I chose the least of the three evils and went back to school. My teacher met me at the door, took me by the arm, and marched me to the rest room where she washed my mouth out with soap.

It was a great lesson. But to be honest, I needed more than a mouth wash. I needed a *heart* wash. My rebellious five-year-old spirit had shown up in my mouth.

As we saw in chapter 1, James refers to the tongue as a bit, a rudder, and a fire (3:3–6). These things are all affected by something else. The horse's bit is controlled by the rider, the rudder is wielded by the helmsman, and the fire is born in the spark. So our tongues march to the drumbeat of our spirits.

Sometimes we are embarrassed when our tongues reveal our inner selves. It's like a slip showing below the hemline of our well-dressed lives. We attempt to appear classy and elegant, but then we open our mouths and our true spirit shows. Some of us don't even realize it! If we knew we were trailing a streamer of toilet paper from a shoe, we would do something about it. But what can we do if we ever realize our tongues are just as embarrassing to us?

One option is to stop talking. "Even a fool, when he keeps silent, is considered wise" (Proverbs 17:28). But that's only a temporary solution because we can't keep quiet forever. I can wire my jaws shut to lose weight, but when I unwire them the weight will return if I haven't changed my eating habits. Weight loss needs more than a shut mouth; it requires inner change. So it is with our speech. Though silence is golden, it is not the key to a transformed tongue.

In nearly every Scripture passage where the tongue is mentioned or illustrated, there is also an insight into the heart problem that prompted the sinful talk. Examining these problems is step one in transforming speech from the inside out, so let's take a look at three "heart problems"—pride, anger, and fear—that create sins of the tongue.

THE PROUD HEART

Spiritually speaking, pride is the elevation of self at the expense of God and His glory. It results in a self-serving lifestyle and takes credit for what God has done and given. "In pride the wicked hotly pursue the afflicted. . . . The

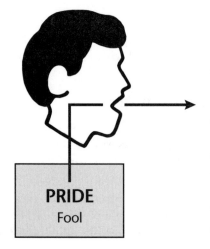

BOASTING
FLATTERY
REVILING
CURSING
LYING
MOCKERY
CONTENTION
SLANDER
GOSSIP
QUARRELING
PERVERSE SPEECH
CARELESS OPINIONS
ANGRY WORDS

PRIDE
Fool

wicked, in the haughtiness of his countenance, does not seek
Him. All his thoughts are, 'There is no God'" (Psalm 10:2, 4).
It's no wonder that "with the mouth of the foolish, ruin is at
hand" (Proverbs 10:14).

Pride is directly connected with negative speech patterns
in a variety of ways:

- Pride and arrogance result in evil behavior and
  perverse speech (Proverbs 8:13).
- Boasting, reviling God, cursing, lying, and contention
  may all result from pride (Psalm 10).
- Flattery is closely related to pride (Psalm 12).
- Proud people slander righteous people (Psalm 59).
- Insolent and arrogant people tend to gossip (Romans
  1:29–30).
- Scoffing, malice, and oppressive threats are by-products
  of a proud spirit (Psalm 73:6–11).
- Pride breeds quarrels (Proverbs 13:10).

When Hannah was found barren, Elkanah's other wife frequently taunted her—year after year. It got to the point where
Hannah couldn't eat and was reduced to tears (1 Samuel
1:6–7). Yet when Hannah finally gave birth to Samuel, she
said a prayer of thanksgiving during which she realized that
the cruel words of her rival came from a proud spirit. She
prayed, "Do not let arrogance come out of your mouth; for
the Lord is a God of knowledge, and with Him actions are
weighed" (2:3).

THE ANGRY HEART

Anger is one of our most powerful emotions. It has the
capacity for destruction on personal, as well as social, levels.
Though anger is vented in many ways, it is often expressed
through our words. Hatred and bitterness are the poisonous
fruit of long-term, unresolved anger.

An angry spirit creates dissension, lying lips, strife, and
threats (Proverbs 10:12, 18; 15:18; 24:28–29; 29:22; 30:33).

Sometimes we threaten others with abusive speech because they make us feel fearful and insecure. Fear of "getting caught" can lead to deceit, if not outright lying. Fear of losing a friendship can result in flattery and exaggeration.

Granted, certain fears and insecurities are part of life. They should point us to God, who is bigger than any of our fears. As our fears get stronger, so should our faith. Spiritual growth and discipline *can* be the result of fear. Unfortunately, many people do not yield their fears to God. As a result, they spin out on a self-oriented "survival track" that leads to frantic and destructive responses. It's not surprising that our speech often reflects such fearful responses.

A NEW HEART

When Dr. Christian Barnard pioneered the first heart transplant surgery, there was great hope for those with heart trouble. Though the technique of *physical* heart transplants is continually being refined, *spiritual* heart transplants are readily available.

When Saul was about to become the first king of Israel, his life and duties were going to change dramatically. During that period of transition, "God gave him another heart" (1 Samuel 10:9 KJV). David acknowledged God's heart-transforming power when he prayed, "Create in me a clean heart, O God, and renew a steadfast spirit within me" (Psalm 51:10). And Paul reminds us, "If any man is in Christ, he is a new creature; the old things passed away; behold, new things have come" (2 Corinthians 5:17).

When we ask God for a new heart and start trying to "clean up our act" verbally, we may be surprised how much cleaning there is to do. A couple of years ago, a woman in Ohio was clearing out her garage as part of a municipal cleanup day. When she tried to remove a pair of tennis shoes from a pile of debris, she was shocked to discover that they were attached to a corpse. Investigators speculated that the body might have been there when the woman moved into the house a year previously. When we start trying to clean up our speech, we may find that much more trash has accumulated than we originally thought.

Expelling the verbal villains of pride, anger, and fear is seldom easy. They are Satan's stranglehold on our spiritual potential for growth and effectiveness. But God can plant genuine humility in the place of pride, patience in the place of anger, and love in the place of fear. Humility, patience, and love reigning in our hearts will stimulate words that are pleasing to God and helpful to those around us.

8

SPEAKING OUT FOR NUMBER ONE

Push Your Pride Aside

One morning I was waiting to be served at my favorite donut shop when a man came in behind me and called out to the approaching clerk, "One small coffee, black."

I was incensed because he could clearly see I was waiting. I decided not to make an issue out of it, but I quietly muttered to the clerk, "I was next." I thought, *This guy is really rude.* But as I fussed over it, I realized he was simply demonstrating the ethic of our culture.

"Looking out for number one" has become a way of life for many people. Self-fulfillment, self-elevation, and self-advancement are priorities that affect our behavior. We can make such concepts sound like modern thought and well-spun philosophies, yet they are little more than alternative forms of *pride*. In recent years, pride has come out of the closet and is parading itself as the truly successful way to live.

At its very core, pride desires to make *self* the most important person in the universe. When Satan was judged by God, it was because of his pride. Satan said in his heart, "I will ascend to heaven; I will raise my throne above the stars of God, and I will sit on the mount of assembly in the recesses of the north. I will ascend above the heights of the clouds; I will make myself like the Most High" (Isaiah 14:13–14). He wanted to be number one.

Pride takes orders only from within, and it seeks to accu-

Peter challenged all Christians to "Humble yourselves under the mighty hand of God" (1 Peter 5:6). God is the ultimate point of authority in the universe. Wise people comprehend this truth and submit to it.

Since humility taps into the strength of God, it allows us to be assertive, bold, and courageous as long as we maintain a tenacious loyalty to serve Him. Consequently, the effects of humility will show in our speech. A person who makes God number one will replace pride-centered words with expressions that:

- Reject unrighteous suggestions and claims.
- Express loyalty to God's will regardless of the cost.
- Worship and praise God for who He is, not just for what He has done.
- Speak God's truth in the face of rebellion and error.
- Encourage others to yield to God's rightful place.

Putting God in His proper place also allows us to relate more effectively with each other. As we humbly submit to God, He then asks us to submit to one another (John 13:34–35). The vertical response of humility (to God) should result in a number of horizontal responses (to others), including:

- Husbands responding to the needs of their wives (Ephesians 5:25–33).
- Wives responding to the headship of their husbands (Ephesians 5:22–24).
- Parents responding to the needs of their children (Ephesians 6:4).
- Children responding to the authority of their parents (Ephesians 6:1).
- Younger men responding to the wisdom of older men (1 Peter 5:5).
- All Christians responding to the needs of one another (Ephesians 5:21), the needs of the world in general

(Galatians 6:10), the Word of God (John 14:21), spiritual leaders (Hebrews 13:17), and governmental authority (Romans 13:1).

The essence of humility is found in Paul's message to the Philippians:

> Do nothing from selfishness or empty conceit, but with humility of mind let each of you regard one another as more important than yourselves; do not merely look out for your own personal interests, but also for the interests of others. Have this attitude in yourselves which was also in Christ Jesus, who, although He existed in the form of God, did not regard equality with God a thing to be grasped, but emptied Himself, taking the form of a bond-servant, and being made in the likeness of men. And being found in appearance as a man, He humbled Himself by becoming obedient to the point of death, even death on a cross. (2:3–8)

Yielding to God in submission will soon result in improved speech habits in our relationship to others. Speech patterns that destroy others will disappear, and in their place will arise words that protect people from damage, express genuine concern, build up others spiritually and emotionally, promote pure thoughts and right relationships, encourage positive thoughts toward God and others, and communicate comfort, love, joy, understanding, encouragement, and peace.

THE GOD-MADE MAN

We often hear praise for the "self-made man" (or woman). Part of the American dream seems to be the ability to pull ourselves up by our own bootstraps. Though not consciously intended to preclude God from His place as ultimate provider, such a concept focuses on our attempts to be self-sufficient.

While God has chosen to include human beings in accomplishing His plan, He remains the ultimate source of all that we have and are. Even though God used Moses and Aaron to lead the Israelites out of Egypt, God Himself was clearly the provider throughout their transfer to the Promised Land. Scripture makes this point clearly:

> In the wilderness He fed you manna which your fathers did not know, that He might humble you and that He might test you, to do good for you in the end. Otherwise, you may say in your heart, "My power and the strength of my hand made me this wealth." But you shall remember the Lord your God, for it is He who is giving you power to make wealth, that He may confirm His covenant which He swore to your fathers, as it is this day. (Deuteronomy 8:16–18)

Before the appearance of manna, Israel went hungry. God brought them to the end of themselves. Then, in the provision of manna, He daily demonstrated that He is the source of provision and life. This humbling lesson was to teach them "that man does not live by bread alone, but man lives by everything that proceeds out of the mouth of the Lord" (v. 3).

God had already told the Israelites, "When the Lord your God brings you into the land which He swore to your fathers, Abraham, Isaac and Jacob, to give you, great and splendid cities which *you did not build,* and houses full of all good things which *you did not fill,* and hewn cisterns which *you did not dig,* vineyards and olive trees which *you did not plant,* and you shall eat and be satisfied, then watch yourself, that you do not forget the Lord who brought you from the land of Egypt, out of the house of slavery" (Deuteronomy 6:10–12, emphasis added).

Self-sufficiency breeds pride. God-sufficiency, on the other hand, breeds a grateful, worshiping spirit. Success sometimes goes to a person's head. Like the Israelites, we are in continual danger of taking for granted the abundant provisions of God. When we forget that all we have and are is because of God, we think more of ourselves than we ought, and we usurp the glory that belongs to Him.

On occasion, God permits suffering instead of success. Humility demands that we submit to God's plan in bad times as well as good. In trying times, pride shakes its fist in God's face. A proud person is unwilling to accept growth and glory through pressure and pain. The advice of Job's wife, "Curse God and die," was the result of a proud spirit (Job 2:9). Job's attitude, however, reflected the courageous strength of humility: "Though He slay me, I will hope in Him" (13:15).

Paul knew what it was like to exercise humility under pressure. He had some kind of impairment, which he referred to as his "thorn in the flesh" (2 Corinthians 12:7). He wrote, "Concerning this I entreated the Lord three times that it might leave me. And He has said to me, 'My grace is sufficient for you, for power is perfected in weakness.' Most gladly, therefore, I will rather boast about my weaknesses, that the power of Christ may dwell in me. Therefore I am well content with weaknesses, with insults, with distresses, with persecutions, with difficulties, for Christ's sake; for when I am weak, then I am strong" (vv. 8–10).

It is important to God that we remain grateful and humble toward Him—whether He places us on Easy Street or leads us through a series of turbulent trials. In fact, as it was with the Israelites in the wilderness, God will often humble us through trials in order to prepare us to better appreciate good times to follow.

Early in my career, a small group of believers made a great financial commitment to allow me to be in ministry full-time. It was a big step of faith for them. What they didn't realize was that it meant our family would have to live on only two-thirds of the income to which we were accustomed. Those were "manna years" for us as the whole family learned that all we are and have is from God.

During those years, God clothed our daughter with beautiful, hardly worn hand-me-downs from a family we had met only once. He kept old cars nearly maintenance-free and answered our prayers when new tires were needed. He frequently surprised us with unexpected income just when we needed it. In fact, my wife and I used to joke that if a little extra money came in, it was God's advance warning that the washer was going to break down. On one occasion, I came home to find a large box from a lady in the church where I had grown up. I hadn't seen her in years. The box contained three suits that had belonged to her son, a businessman in Arizona. All three were in perfect condition. They were exactly what I would have picked out in a store, and they fit me to a tee. No alterations needed!

For believers with a handle on reality, acknowledging God as the ultimate provider brings the joy of a humble spirit. It translates into freedom and the esteem of feeling good about ourselves because God is working in us and through us. It is reflected in our character, conviction, and conversation.

That's not to say that developing ongoing humility is easy. Many of us take the attitude of the Mac Davis song, "It's Hard to Be Humble (When You're Perfect in Every Way)." We realize, of course, that we're not perfect, yet we frequently act as if we are. No doubt that's what T. S. Eliot was getting at when he wrote, "Humility is the most difficult of all virtues to achieve; nothing dies harder than the desire to think well of oneself."

An extreme example of "acting" humble without feeling genuine humility took place recently in London. A pedestrian was waiting to cross the street, and a car slowed to let him go across. However, the pedestrian failed to acknowledge the "humble" graciousness of the driver—so the driver got out of his car and attacked him, breaking his cheekbone with a scaffolding pole. Before driving off, the driver screamed, "Next time say 'thank you'!" From all appearances, the driver wanted to be perceived as humble and willing to put others first, yet he apparently wanted full credit for every act of humility he performed. Humility, by his definition, did nothing to affect his actions or his words.

Yielding to the reality of God's work as provider and sustainer will reflect positively in our speech. We will:

- Give God credit for what we are, what we have, and what we have accomplished.
- Give God credit for the good we see in others.
- Encourage others to recognize God's place as sovereign provider in their lives.

• Reflect spirits of gratefulness to God in every circumstance.

Humility gladly submits to God's rightful place as Lord. It produces a right spirit toward others and a grateful sense of submission to God's provision on our behalf. A living commitment to humility revolutionizes our speech. It causes us to consistently speak out for the *real* number one.

9

DEFUSING ANGER

Douse the Fire in Your Tongue

The story is told of an elementary teacher who patiently put boots on thirty-two students before sending them out into the snow. As the last boot was going onto the thirty-second student, the child said, "These aren't my boots." The teacher, by now out of patience, furiously ripped off the boots. The child then continued, "They are my sister's boots, but she let me wear them today."

We all know the adage that patience is a virtue. But we rarely consider the opposite: anger can be a vice. Anger takes over when patience runs out and often vents itself in harsh words. Angry words are the noxious smoke from the fire in our hearts. Henry Ward Beecher said it well: "Speak when you are angry, and you'll make the best speech you'll ever regret."

Scripture is filled with illustrations of angry words and the problems they cause. Anger was Cain's response after God rejected his sacrifice (Genesis 4:5). King Saul's anger was kindled when David received more praise than he did from the people (1 Samuel 18:5–9). Jonah's anger was kindled against God when God didn't perform as Jonah expected (Jonah 4). In the parable of the prodigal son, the elder son spoke angrily to his father because he felt he had been treated unfairly (Luke 15:11–32). And the disciples became indignant after the mother of James and John asked for positions of power and prestige for her sons (Matthew 20:20–28).

Unfortunately, anger never lives in isolation. It is like a cancer that continues to grow and spread. It may begin with just a small incident of rejection, jealousy, disappointment, thwarted gain, or unkind comparison. But if these little things aren't resolved, anger can grow into other problems.

Cain's rejected offering sparked the murder of his brother, which resulted in fear, alienation, and God's judgment. King Saul's anger caused him to brood, become depressed, and develop a deep hatred for David. Jonah's anger turned inward and Godward as he became vulnerable to self-pity, depression, and thoughts of suicide. The elder son's anger alienated him from his father, who was the source of his sustenance and future inheritance. And the disciples' anger resulted in division and strife during a time when they desperately needed to be unified.

Anger becomes a social problem with far-reaching effects when it vents itself through words. How can we prevent anger from blocking our constructive words of peace and reconciliation? We need to replace an angry spirit with a patient spirit. The New Testament uses two primary words for *patience.* One carries the thought of not returning harm to those who have harmed us, even though it is within our power to do so. The other word reflects the ability to maintain a good attitude even while under pressure.

Both dimensions of patience contradict our natural reactions. When we're offended, hurt, or reproved, we want to retaliate. And when we feel the pressure of life, we pray for relief instead of the grace to endure the difficult situation. We are like wet watermelon seeds under someone's thumb— we tend to quickly squirt out at the least bit of pressure. If we can't escape the pressure, we become angry with the forces that hold us there.

God's Word tells us how to achieve both dimensions of patience rather than fostering an angry spirit. Unfortunately, some people have let their anger go unchecked for so long that it is deeply ingrained in them. These are what we term "angry people." Counseling sessions with a biblically sensitive Christian therapist may be necessary to deal effectively with such long-standing anger. But even "angry people" can find important insights from God's Word that, when applied, bring awareness, sensitivity, and peace.

To begin with, we must realize that anger is a valid, God-given emotion. God is sinless, yet Scripture tells us He possesses the capacity to become angry. Anger is a "signal emotion" that alerts us to injustice, ungodliness, and unrighteousness. It helps us know right from wrong.

Even though God intended anger to be a righteous response to something that's wrong, we all have felt anger that is far from righteous. The task of the growing believer is to separate anger from the sins that often accompany it. We should be alert to our anger, and then allow it to move us to constructive responses. If we act instinctively without thinking, anger can intensify into abusive, violent, self-destructive responses. But if we learn to identify and respond to our anger, it can stimulate prayer, concern, corrective action, and a deep trust in God that permits us to love our enemies and enjoy inner peace.

Three commands in the New Testament enable us to respond constructively to anger. All three involve the application of patience.

1. *Be slow to anger* (James 1:19). This habit develops our ability to handle anger when it first begins to rise. It equips us to evaluate what has happened and choose appropriate responses.
2. *Do not sin* (Ephesians 4:26). We must be aware of the sins that so easily attach themselves to anger. Recognizing such potential problems equips us to resist them.
3. *Deal with anger before sundown* (Ephesians 4:26). We can learn to resolve anger by directing our focus toward God and our constructive energy toward the source of the anger. The goal should be to expedite positive responses that bring inner peace and healing.

The rest of this chapter will deal with the first two of these commands. The following chapter will offer some suggestions for dealing with anger before it gets out of hand.

HESITATE AND EVALUATE

James's command to be *slow to anger* (1:19) is the biblical equivalent of our traditional "count to ten" routine. Literally, the word *slow* means to hesitate or delay. The essence of this wise advice is to be patient. It urges us to wait with a good spirit while seeking a constructive response to the pressure we feel. Restraining anger means hesitating long enough to carefully evaluate the situation.

There are at least five things we can do to help us hesitate, evaluate, and control our anger:

1. *Remember God's statements to angry people.* If we pay attention, we can learn from the mistakes of others without making those same mistakes ourselves. We can find numerous examples of how God dealt with angry people in the past. Below are three such examples, along with the comments we would be wise to consider at the onset of anger.

- "Why are you angry? . . . If you do well, will not your countenance be lifted up?" These were God's questions to Cain (Genesis 4:6–7). Cain's anger was his response to reproof in a situation where he was clearly wrong. When we find ourselves in similar situations, we must honestly evaluate the circumstances, humbly repent, and seek to do what is right. Anger will then diffuse into patient, submissive reconciliation.

- "Do you have good reason to be angry?" When Jonah wanted to watch God obliterate the Ninevites, this was God's challenge to the prophet (Jonah 4:4). Jonah showed little evidence of mercy, and he expected God to feel the same way and perform according to his own desires. But Nineveh was God's responsibility. Assuming responsibility that doesn't belong to us frequently creates unnecessary anger. Continually submitting to God's will, though sometimes unpleasant for us, develops the patience that will produce words of loyalty and expressions that reflect His grace.

- "Son, you have always been with me, and all that is mine is yours" (Luke 15:31). You might recognize this phrase from the parable of the prodigal son, spoken by the father to the jealous older brother. When we seek to find satisfaction by comparing ourselves to others, the result is frequently self-pity and anger, because we ignore all the good things for which we should be grateful. At the first hint of anger, we ought to determine whether our anger grows out of a self-centered, unloving comparison with others. Granted, it is sometimes difficult to "rejoice with those who rejoice" (Romans 12:15), but a continued focus on all we have to be grateful for will quell anger and discontentment.

2. Check to see if you have sufficient facts to justify your anger. Seeking to understand both sides of a matter not only slows anger but also reflects itself in words that show self-control and a fair spirit.

3. Try to understand the situation from other points of view. Often, mentally placing yourself in the environment of the one who has made you angry defuses the anger and kindles a spirit of tolerance. If you look hard enough, you'll usually find reasons to explain the other person's less-than-desirable behavior. This kind of patience is called gentleness (Galatians 5:23).

4. Pinpoint the specific cause of anger. The sooner you get to the source, the better you will be able to deal with it. The chart on page 105 lists ten common sources of anger and some simple steps to take to begin to deal with the problem.

5. Verbalize the sense of oncoming anger. It's amazing how effective it is to honestly admit that you are feeling angry, but it isn't easy to do so. We are normally defensive about our feelings. Pride makes it hard to say, "I am angry." If I am a little "hot under the collar" about something and my wife asks, "Why are you so angry?" my retort may be a quick and heated, "I'm not angry!" Such a response is not only dishonest, but it is also likely to stir up anger in my wife as well. I always

The patience to hesitate, evaluate, and reject anger-spawned sins puts a lid on the flames. It gives us the opportunity to transform the destructive force of our anger into words that are tastefully seasoned, enjoyable to hear, and a positive contribution to the health of those around us.

SOURCE OF ANGER	APPLICATION OF PATIENCE
Stress from an unorganized life or a life that is overcommitted to low-priority involvements	Organize. Quit low-priority involvements and practice saying "No" once a day.
Slothful patterns that leave important matters undone or unfinished	Work hard at priority matters.
Personal guilt	Seek forgiveness from God and others. Begin to apply principles of victory to that particular weakness.
Righteousness and justice violated	Commit judgment to God (Romans 12:17–21) and turn the energy of your anger into constructive resolution of the problem.
Symbolic anger—transferring anger from past nonrelated incidents that remind you of the present situation	Recognize the sin of bitterness in your own heart (Hebrews 12:15). Understand that it is unfair to punish someone because of the past mistakes of others. If necessary, seek the help of a competent counselor.
Residual anger—unresolved situations from previously repeated incidents	Deal with the recurring problem at a neutral time with open, nondefensive communication. Seek the help of a competent, neutral third party if necessary.
Unfulfilled expectations	Determine to glorify God (Philippians 1:19–20).
Rights violated	Yield your rights to God, who will provide for all your needs. If necessary, appeal to the proper authorities (government, parents, boss, and so on).
Imposed crises that are out of your control	Trust the sovereign design of God and submit to His plan. Seek creative ways to glorify God in the suffering.
Thwarted plans and dreams for self-advancement	Evaluate the true value of the dreams in relation to eternal values. Submit to God's wise plan for your life.

10

PATIENCE APPLIED

Good Words for Bad Deeds

Have you ever set off a burglar alarm accidentally? I did once. One early morning, I turned the key in the door of my church without thinking and almost had a coronary on the spot. Bells began to clang. The entire neighborhood was jolted awake too early on a Sunday morning. Thinking the police would probably be on their way, I panicked and lost all former knowledge of how to shut off the alarm!

Anger is like that. Unsuspectingly, a key is turned in our lives and the blaring alarm goes off both inside and out. We panic and tighten up. The tranquility of the people around us is shattered. Unfortunately, we have no idea how to stop it.

An alarm is not meant to clang on forever and ever. Once it does its job, it needs to be turned off. Otherwise it becomes a major source of frustration and conflict for all who are within earshot. (Just ask any New York City resident who endures almost constant car alarms throughout the night.) An alarm that never shuts off is simply an annoyance.

As I said in the last chapter, anger is like an alarm. It alerts us so we can respond constructively. But after we take time to evaluate what's wrong and deal with the problem without sinning, we must put the anger away.

I am thankful that God understands how difficult it can be for us to extinguish our anger. It often takes time and determined spiritual discipline to release our feelings and allow God to take over. God graciously gives us time to deal with the situation, yet He expects us to start each day fresh, with no unresolved anger carried over from the day before (Ephesians 4:26).

Other passages reinforce the importance of putting anger to rest quickly. For example, we are challenged to "cease from anger and forsake wrath" (Psalm 37:8), and to "let all bitterness and wrath and anger and clamor and slander be put away . . . along with all malice" (Ephesians 4:31).

If we don't rid ourselves of anger, we risk damaging our own reputations as well as those who are the targets of our anger. A few years ago, a high school yearbook editor in Indiana didn't let go of her anger quite soon enough. Just before the yearbook went to press, she defaced the pictures of several girls she didn't like (blacking out teeth, penciling in armpit hair, and so on). After her actions were discovered, the school attempted to recall the five hundred yearbooks. In the aftermath of her anger-inspired actions, the editor suffered more embarrassment than any of her "victims." One of the targets of her anger said, "I was kind of mad that she did it, but we all laughed about it." She then explained that the editor "gets very jealous and mad at people for stupid reasons" and that she "has a big problem when guys go out with other girls after they've gone out with her."

So the victims felt anger for a short time but were soon able to see the humor in the situation. In contrast, when the editor felt anger building for her rivals, she would have done well to have dealt with it one day sooner. Her angry action brought her a lot of attention, but it was probably not what she had in mind. In the end, she was the one who looked like a fool. Unrestrained anger often has a way of manifesting itself in ways far worse than we might imagine.

At the other extreme are people who think good Christians should never feel angry, so they try to repress anger and pretend it doesn't exist. This is not only unscriptural and dishonest, but also physiologically and psychologically dangerous. As someone well said, "When I repress my emotions, my stomach keeps score." People who frequently repress anger become like time bombs just waiting to explode.

Therapists have realized this for years. For a while it was popular to go to extremes to ventilate repressed anger—to let it *all* out by yelling, screaming, swearing, or beating the stuffing out of pillows to feel better. Such actions might have brought momentary relief, but many people soon regretted the words and actions of their rage. Seeds of resentment and distrust were planted in the hearts of those victimized by such ventilation. In addition, subsequent studies indicated that people who were prone to vent their rage tended to become more, not less, angry. Indeed, venting anger addresses the symptom but doesn't get to the source of the problem.

God's Word commands us to deal decisively with our anger. We shouldn't bottle it up, nor should we carelessly vent it at will. A composite understanding of Scripture reveals that turning off our anger requires redirecting our focus and our energy.

REDIRECTING OUR FOCUS

When we become angry, our natural tendency is to direct our mental and emotional focus toward the *source* of our anger. The person who has stimulated the anger becomes an overriding preoccupation. We think about the perceived injustice everywhere we go, so we take it out on other people who have done nothing to deserve our anger. We plan what to say the next time we see the offending person, what he or she might say in reply, and what our follow-up comment will be. We fantasize various schemes of revenge. Meanwhile, in doing all these things, we actually become servants to the one(s) on whom we have focused our anger. The other person may not even know we're angry, and even if he does, the matter doesn't consume his time and energy nearly as much as it does our own.

The intensity of our emotions will usually progress through five stages. At first, we will *fret* about the problem. To fret is to anxiously mull it over in our minds. The fretting will then mature into *envy*. Perhaps we will be jealous of how nicely our wives treat others or of how much time our husbands spend at the office. Envy quickly turns to *anger,* which is the "slow burn." Anger, when permitted to remain, sours into *wrath* (the explosion), and wrath may mature into an actual plot to carry out revenge, which is the stage of *evil.*

The evil we do is not so much because we are nasty people; rather, it is to protect us from further offense, to carry out justice, and to force change in the behavior patterns of those who hurt us. Many times we use words to express our evil response—words that threaten, wound, belittle, and heap guilt on the one causing our pain.

Let's see how the cycle of fret-envy-anger-wrath-evil might work in an everyday situation. Suppose a wife has mentioned to her husband that she feels their marriage could use more romance. In response, the husband offers to take her out to a romantic dinner for two. She feels, however, that she would rather prepare the dinner in the candlelit intimacy of their own home. The next morning, as he goes out the door, she reminds him: "Dinner for two at seven o'clock." He replies, "I can't wait." When the children come home from school, the wife feeds them and sends them to bed early. The table is set. The food smells fantastic. There's a fire in the fireplace, and soft music is playing. The candles are lit. It's seven o'clock. The wife has worked hard to make this a special night. Put yourself in her place as time passes and the husband doesn't show up:

- 7:10—FRET: She wonders what has happened. A traffic jam? An accident?

- 7:30—ENVY: If it had been an accident, the police would have notified her by now. She thinks, *This is how much I'm worth. His business gets more time than I do—and more respect. If this had been a business appointment, he wouldn't have been late, or at least he would have called.*

- 7:45—ANGER: She begins to feel tense and hostile, moving well into the slow burn.

• 8:00—WRATH: As she hears the car pulling into the driveway, she quickly scrapes the food off her plate and puts the empty plate back on the table. Then she takes his plate of food and holds it in the freezer to make it as cold as possible before he comes in.

• 8:03—EVIL: As he walks in the door, he gets what he deserves (or more accurately, what she feels he deserves). The treatment may be varied—silence, a verbal outburst, tears, limited cold conversation, or whatever she feels will be most effective.

The wife has a right to be angry because her husband has been insensitive and irresponsible. (He could have at least called.) Yet when confronted with a level-4 (wrath) or level-5 (evil) reaction, the husband is likely to become defensive. Instead of humbly repenting, he may take a less constructive option: clamming up, turning around and leaving, or standing his ground and fighting. But whatever option he chooses, all hope for revival of romance between them will be postponed.

As common as this downward cycle of anger is, there is a much better course of pursuit provided in Psalm 37. The psalmist knew what it was like to be the victim of "evildoers" and "wrongdoers" (v. 1). Yet he tells us that fretting, envy, anger, wrath, and evildoing are all out of bounds from God's point of view (vv. 1, 8). In their place, he provides five *positive* responses that liberate our focus from the source of our anger and redirect it to God, who is the ultimate solution to our anger. These steps are to trust (v. 3), delight (v. 4), commit (v. 5), rest (v. 7), and wait patiently (v. 7). Let's take a closer look at each one.

Trust

Trusting God means depending on four firm realities that are rooted in God's character and His Word:

1. God is just. Whenever wrong is done, He is acutely aware of it because justice is of absolute importance to Him.

2. God's Word promises that He will repay the wrongs that have been done.

3. God promises to effectively work to change the lives of those who do wrong.

4. God seeks to protect those who trust in Him.

These realities are based on passages such as Genesis 18:25; Romans 12:17–21; Hebrews 12:5–11; and Proverbs 3:11–12; 18:10. As we trust God in these four dimensions, we feel a diminished desire to retaliate, even the score, effect change, or protect ourselves. We begin to realize that these are God's responsibilities. The first step of focusing on God during times of anger is believing that He is at work and putting our trust in Him rather than ourselves.

Delight

This step has two aspects to be considered. First, we are reminded in Scripture that God brings trials into our lives to refine and mature us (James 1). If we keep in mind that pressure builds character, we can accept the burdens in our lives as positive instruments in the hand of God. Despite the hardships, we can learn to acknowledge and appreciate the growth that comes as a result of trials.

The second aspect of this step is the delight we can have from knowing God will work in the lives of our offenders. Many times it is amazing to see how God leads our persecutors into repentance and restoration. And even when people don't respond to God's mercy, we can delight in the fact that eventually God will see that justice is done.

Commit

After successfully trusting and delighting, you can expect Satan to whisper in your ear, "Are you going to let them get away with that?" Or perhaps your friends will say, "You're becoming a pushover—fight back!" When I am angry and offended, I must recommit myself time and time again to focus on God. If I am offended at 7:45, I can mentally trust God and delight in Him right away. But as my mind keeps wandering away from Him and back toward the offense, I need to commit myself to focus on God again at 8:05, 8:07, and 9:23.

Rest

When you have followed the previous three steps, a sense of stillness and peace will begin to reside in your spirit. As long as you are trusting, delighting in, and committing yourself to the Lord, inner peace will be your reward. By transferring the problem to God, your anger has done its job and now you can turn it off.

Wait Patiently

As time passes, it may be difficult to keep your focus on God. Injustice, especially against oneself, has a way of absorbing our thoughts and energy. Time is on the side of our old, sinful natures, attempting to pull us back into the bondage of the offender. If God does not work as quickly as we would like, we tend to revert back to the old fret-envy-anger-wrath-evil cycle. Waiting patiently means committing to these five steps regardless of God's timing.

We must recognize that God's work will not be ultimately completed until the final judgment. In the meantime, maintaining a focus on Him enables us to enjoy peace, a clear conscience, and a deepening maturity in our experience. Our commitment should be based on our desire to obey Him, not dependent on His immediate action on our behalf.

Sally committed herself to these principles after discovering her husband had been having an affair with their babysitter. Though it was difficult to forgive him and keep her anger in check, she eventually experienced peace, a clear conscience, and the maturity that the process brings. As a part of her commitment to keep her anger in check, she memorized Psalm 37:1–11. But one night she succumbed to the temptation to shift the focus back to her husband. As you can imagine, it ignited an internal explosion that was vented through angry words. She told me later that she was enjoying the luxury of the verbal venting when suddenly the words of

Psalm 37 flashed across her mind like a neon sign. She was reminded to trust, delight, commit, rest, and wait patiently. "It took all the fun out of my angry tirade," she confessed. After she regrouped, the peace of trusting in God became fresh to her again. Keeping our focus on God triggers the patience that withholds retaliation.

REDIRECTING OUR ENERGY

As we learn to redirect our focus from the problem situation to God, we also need to redirect our energy. This step involves using the energy that comes with anger for constructive resolution. Successfully dealing with anger requires not only that we transfer the situation to God, but also that we take positive action toward the source of our anger.

We are told to "trust in the Lord and do good" (Psalm 37:3), and this command encompasses at least four crucial responses.

Positive Actions

Forgiveness is possible when I believe that God will deal with my offender and use the offense in a positive way in my life. Every time I am reminded of the source of my anger, it becomes an opportunity to commit myself again to focus on God and consider new ways to heal the division (Ephesians 4:31–32; 1 Peter 2:19–25).

Genuine forgiveness is more than simply giving someone a break after he or she has offended you. We are challenged to then take another step and actually try to show love to the offending party:

> Never pay back evil for evil to anyone. Respect what is right in the sight of all men. If possible, so far as it depends on you, be at peace with all men. Never take your own revenge, beloved, but leave room for the wrath of God, for it is written, "Vengeance is Mine, I will repay," says the Lord. "But if your enemy is hungry, feed him, and if he is thirsty, give him a drink; for in so doing you will heap burning coals on his head." Do not be overcome by evil, but overcome evil with good. (Romans 12:17–21)

Paul is speaking here about the depth of love that meets genuine need. Being sensitive to the needs of those who oppose us is the essence of Christ's exhortation to "love your enemies" (Matthew 5:44). Meeting an enemy's needs and praying for him are strong forms of therapy.

Honest Reactions

Next, we must redirect our energy by honestly communicating with the one who has hurt us. This is not always easy, but if we are truly committed to letting God handle the situation and the offender, we can say what we feel without appearing judgmental. When we communicate with our offenders, we should keep several points in mind to prevent the other person(s) from becoming defensive.

- *Show wisdom in choosing a time and place to talk.* It is usually unwise to confront the offender while he is doing something that bothers you. But later you might invite him out for coffee to discuss how his actions make you feel.

- *Carefully choose words that communicate an open and nondefensive attitude.* Don't allow your anger to cause you to jump to conclusions. Ask questions that give people a chance to explain their point of view. For example, you might ask, "What did you have in mind when you said that to me?"

- *Have the humility to admit your part in the problem.* This will often enable the other person to admit his short-comings as well.

- *State your perception of the situation without projecting blame.* Encourage others to understand you before forcefully attempting to sway them to your way of thinking.

- *Commit yourself not to permit the conversation to deteriorate into a revival of anger.* Don't let a few cross words from the other person set you off. Anyone can get into a petty argument. It takes spiritual maturity to keep

anger at bay during the discussion so you can arrive at a
mutually satisfying conclusion.

Maintain your commitment to the trust-delight-commit-
rest-wait patiently perspective so that even if the other person
refuses to listen and cooperate, your trust is still in the Lord
to intercede. This is crucial to blocking the reentry of anger
into your spirit.

Responsible Reaction

Taking responsibility to actively right the wrong is an
important step in redirecting our energy. God has ordained
certain authorities to exercise discipline toward those who
have been unjust and unrighteous. Government, the church,
parents, and employers are all recognized channels of
authority. An appeal to any of these authorities is legitimate
when the offense is something that involves them. However,
we must remember that God has many additional unseen
options to accomplish His work of justice and discipline. Any
step toward personal involvement should be done with
prayer, discernment, and patience.

Exhaustion Reaction

Physical activity can also be a constructive way to redirect
anger. I have a friend who jogs and meditates on the positive
ways he can approach problems. Some people clean their
entire house with the residual energy of their anger. House-
cleaning gives good opportunity to pray and plan for helpful
responses as well.

Redirecting our focus and our energy gives birth to
patience in our hearts. Patience rejects angry words and
replaces them with words that:

- Reflect a forgiving spirit.
- Are constructive.
- Lead to resolution.

- Are nonjudgmental.
- Reflect a confidence in God's ultimate resolution of the problem.
- Are sensitively timed.
- Are sensitive to the needs of others, even the needs of our offenders.
- Allow a peaceful silence for God to do His work.
- Testify to the positive hope of God's work in our lives as well as the lives of our offenders.

The words of others can be cruel and hurtful. Within the last couple of weeks I read about yet another teenager who committed suicide because her peers taunted her with rude comments about her weight. Unfortunately, this type of tragedy is becoming all too common. But it reminded me of a 1993 account of a ten-year-old boy in Minnesota. He was persistently harassed by about a dozen other boys who had started calling him sexually explicit names. The teasing had been going on since first grade, but their comments had only recently taken on a sexual tone. In response, the boy first tried telling them to shut up or hitting back. Later he enlisted the help of school authorities, but they didn't believe him. Yet, rather than giving up, he took a tape recorder to school and got his own proof about the verbal insults. As a result, five of the other boys were suspended and a complaint was brought against the school for failing to protect the third-grader.

It's not exactly a model of turning the other cheek, but the patience of the boy in dealing with an ongoing problem is to be commended. It certainly beats the tragic alternative that some young people choose. If we as adults are as patient and persistent in dealing with the people who pester us, perhaps we can restore some relationships.

Patience is the virtue that transforms an angry tongue. Patience takes time to hesitate and evaluate. It rejects anger sins. True patience finds its strength in an unflinching focus on God and an unconditional love toward those who have hurt us.

11

THE TRUST-LOVE LIFE

Conquer Fear with Love

Fear cripples us emotionally. As a little boy, I sometimes found it hard to sleep because I was afraid of the dark. That fear played all kinds of tricks on me: clothes on the chair looked like a monster in the shadows; snakes and alligators could be under my bed; and who knew what lay just out of reach between my sheets? I had no relief until my father would hear my call and come turn on the lights. The light dispelled the darkness and canceled the fear.

We never outgrow our vulnerability to fear. It continues to paralyze our spirits so that we are like kids hiding under the covers—unable to do what we know we should. Fear saps our spiritual vitality and diminishes our willingness to speak words of courage and love. We become afraid to tell others about Christ, to exercise our spiritual gifts, to extend our lives and resources for the benefit of others, and to venture into new areas of growth and discovery.

Fear also leaves us vulnerable to Satan's attacks. If a young woman is afraid of losing her boyfriend, she may do things she knows are opposed to God's will. Fear of separation and the unknown has kept many people from pursuing missions opportunities. Fear of losing prestige, money, power, status, and friends has caused some to compromise biblical convictions and a righteous standing before God. Satan uses fear to pull the strings of our lives, and it seems that many strings are attached to our tongues.

What will enable us to transform our fearful words into words of love and courage? What is the biblical cure for a fearful spirit? There are two steps we can take to topple fear from the throne of our existence—we must learn to trust and to love.

Emotionally, fear is self-centered. It exists because I want to protect and preserve myself. At times this kind of fear can be constructive. Fear of getting burned keeps a child from putting his or her hand on a hot stove. A healthy fear of wild animals while camping prevents us from trying to pet grizzly bears. But fear also surfaces frequently in destructive ways. When others interfere with our plans and threaten the fulfillment of our desires, we may verbally intimidate or abuse them in an attempt to remove them as obstacles.

What corrals and transforms this self-centered fear? We are told that *love* casts out fear—the "perfect" love that commits itself to God's will and others' needs (1 John 4:18). Yet trust must precede love. If I wrongly assume I am solely responsible for protecting and preserving all that God has given me, then I will be dominated by fear. I am incapable of standing alone against outside forces that threaten my present existence or future dreams, because these forces are greater than I am. I can only dispel my fear by trusting in God to protect me and provide for me as He sees fit (Psalm 56:3). As I learn to trust in God to care for me, I become free from self-interest and better able to love and care for others.

Witnessing to my lost friends requires trusting in God's power to convince and convict. Sharing financially to help someone else requires trusting in God's promise to meet my own needs. Obeying God during times when I'd much rather chart my own course requires trusting in His wisdom and love for me.

Activating a biblical blend of trust and love is the key to overcoming fear. It is the prerequisite to words of courage and grace.

THE TRUST FACTOR

As we have seen in previous chapters, the Israelites murmured and complained after the ten spies brought their report from the Promised Land. Rahab lied to the soldiers in Jericho. Peter cursed, swore, and denied the Lord in the courtyard of the chief priest. Why?

In each case, people were locked in to the fear of godless self-concern, and their fear showed in their words. Each of them could have chosen to trust God to deliver them, which would have given courageous testimony to their faith. All of them knew God had frequently proven His ability to deliver His people. Yet they lapsed into the false assumption that it was up to them to protect themselves.

In contrast, Shadrach, Meshach, and Abednego demonstrated tremendous trust in God as they faced the fiery furnace. They revealed no hint of self-concern. They expressed their confidence in God to bring them safely through the ordeal and even affirmed their trust in Him if He chose not to (Daniel 3:16–18). Their trust was unconditional, and their words reflected their resolve that God was worthy to be worshiped and served, regardless of the outcome.

The psalmist declared, "When I am afraid, I will put my trust in You. In God, whose word I praise, in God I have put my trust; I shall not be afraid. What can mere man do to me? . . . Then my enemies will turn back in the day when I call; this I know, that God is for me. In God, whose word I praise, in the Lord, whose word I praise, in God I have put my trust, I shall not be afraid. What can man do to me?" (Psalm 56:3–4, 9–11).

God's character provides four handles for us to hold on to in the face of fear: the reality of God's presence, power, protection, and provision. These four things form a strong foundation for our trust.

The Presence of God

When I was a boy, our family visited a church in one of the most dangerous sections of New York City. It was an evening service, and it was already getting dark when we arrived. We parked a block away, and as we walked, I became more and more afraid. Thankfully, we made it safely to the church and enjoyed the service. Afterward, the pastor asked two of his deacons to escort us back to the car. Because of their large size, they looked like the church "bouncers." Though it was completely dark by that time, I had no fear. What made the difference? The presence of those who could protect me.

Scripture is full of reminders to trust in the presence of God during times of fear. Joshua was commanded not to be terrified because "the Lord your God is with you wherever you go" (Joshua 1:9). In the shepherd's psalm, we are told to fear no evil because God is with us (Psalm 23:4). The book of Hebrews also encourages an attitude of boldness: "He Himself has said, 'I will never desert you, nor will I ever forsake you,' so that we confidently say, 'The Lord is my helper, I will not be afraid. What will man do to me?'" (13:5–6).

The Power of God

God has unlimited power, and He delights in sharing it on behalf of His people. His power dwells within us to enable us to witness (Acts 1:8). It dwells in His Word to convict and transform us (Hebrews 4:12). The power of God is used to supply our needs (Philippians 4:19); to give us strength in trouble (2 Corinthians 12:8–10); to keep us from temptations and trials that would be beyond our ability to handle (1 Corinthians 10:13); and to provide escape mechanisms in those temptations that He does permit (10:13). The strength of God can disarm any intimidating influence in our environment. "God hath not given us the spirit of fear; but of power, and of love, and of a sound mind" (2 Timothy 1:7 KJV).

The Protection of God

Scripture clearly portrays God as a protector. Israel was protected many times against military opponents who were far superior. Jesus Christ walked untouched through hostile mobs. Though frequently God permits His people to experience suffering (Hebrews 11:35–38), He activates His protecting power when that is in the best interest of His plan.

Many of God's protective interventions have been dramatic. His protection of Abraham's wife was especially so (Genesis 20). When Sarah was added to King Abimelech's harem, God protected her by closing all the wombs of the king's house and striking the king deathly ill. God takes special delight in protecting those who trust Him. When He chooses not to remove us from troubling circumstances, He still protects us with His grace to cope with the situation (2 Corinthians 12:7–10).

Psalm 91 pictures God as a protecting refuge: "He who dwells in the shelter of the Most High will abide in the shadow of the Almighty. I will say to the Lord, 'My refuge and my fortress, my God, in whom I trust!'" (vv. 1–2).

The Provision of God

God provides all we need to go through circumstances that would normally defeat us with fear. He supplies us with His Word, which assures us of the fullness of His character and gives us instructions that really work. He provides the support of fellow believers who pray for us and with us. We also have access to His indwelling Spirit, who prays for us, guides us, teaches us, and provides the assurance that He will meet all of our needs.

The kind of trust that evaporates fear is a committed trust—not in ourselves, but in God's presence, shared power, protection, and provision. This level of trust will be reinforced by words of courage, loyalty, and commitment regardless of the situations we face. A trusting heart eliminates doubting, murmuring, anger, lying, jealousy, slander, and gossip. In the place of these verbal sins, trust allows us to use words that:

- Affirm commitment to righteousness at all cost.
- Give testimony to God's sufficiency.

- Express confidence and loyalty to God regardless of the circumstance.
- Express truth in the face of danger.
- Encourage others to experience the presence, power, protection, and provision of God.
- Forgive those who hurt and misuse us.
- Express gratefulness to God and those who provide support as we face difficult times.
- Give testimony to our experiences of deliverance and grace.

THE LOVE FACTOR

As our trust in God increases, we find ourselves better able to love Him, which in turn helps us love others. Love and fear are mutually exclusive: "There is no fear in love; but perfect love casts out fear" (1 John 4:18). Fear, as we have said, is self-centered, but true love focuses on the needs of others. Therefore, love is unquestionably more powerful than fear.

God's Word speaks of a deep love that is far superior to any of our cultural impressions of what love should be. Divine love is sensitive to real needs and motivates us to extend our resources to meet those needs (John 3:16; Romans 5:8). Christ has loved us with divine love, and we are to love one another with that same kind of love (John 15:9–13). This degree of love is even able to conquer the fear of death.

Divine love is unconditional; it is not offered in response to someone or something. By definition, God is love (1 John 4:8). Therefore, the love He extends to us has nothing to do with who we are or how we act. He loves us from within Himself. This is why the Cross is possible. Jesus Christ died for us, not because we are worthy, but because He is love.

Jesus also said, "This is My commandment, that you love one another, just as I have loved you" (John 15:12). Our love for one another, then, is to reflect God's divine love. We are supposed to show concern and care for others because we possess God's kind of love and we extend it to all—unconditionally, regardless of their worth and value.

In *Mere Christianity*, C. S. Lewis says that the "worldly man treats certain people kindly because he likes them; the Christian, trying to treat everyone kindly, finds himself liking more and more people as he goes—including people he could not even have imagined himself liking at the beginning" (*The Best of C. S. Lewis*, The Iversen Associates, p. 505).

Divine love is not an emotional response, but an act of the will. We *choose* to love others. If we wait to "feel" like loving someone, the love we display will be erratic and arbitrary. We possess the ability to give to the needs of others regardless of how we feel because "the love of God has been poured out within our hearts" (Romans 5:5).

The more we love others, the better we will feel about them and about ourselves. Where our treasures are, there our hearts will be as well (Matthew 6:21). When we invest our treasures of time, prayers, and resources into a loving relationship, our hearts soon follow and warm the friendship. Divine love stimulates right feelings.

And in demonstrating this degree of love to other people, we simultaneously display our love for God. We prove our love for Him by willfully sharing His concern for people (1 John 5:3). Divine love is the badge of our discipleship (John 13:34–35). The dual nature of divine love—loving God and loving others—is evident in Christ's statement that we are to love God with all our beings and to love our neighbors as ourselves (Matthew 22:34–39).

Genuine love drives out fear because it turns our attention upward and outward—toward the concerns of God and the needs of others. As we get involved with others, fear no longer thrives on our self-centered concern for our own welfare. When I trust God in every circumstance, I am free to commit myself in love to the concerns of God and the needs of others without thinking of myself.

A commitment to active divine love beautifully improves our speech habits. One of our greatest capacities to meet needs is using the right words to express encouragement from a loving, caring heart. Unfortunately, we usually tend to speak empty words and phrases that reflect polite concern while keeping a person's needs at a safe distance. We ask "How are you?" when we don't *really* care. We must remember the warning of 1 Corinthians 13:1, "If I speak with the tongues of men and of angels, but do not have love, I have become a noisy gong or a clanging cymbal."

The same chapter of Scripture lists fourteen characteristics of true love. These are the things we should look for to determine whether or not we have true love. They will become evident through pleasant, gracious words that are dynamically used by God to heal, warm, encourage, and excite others to righteousness and faith. The chart on pages 128–29 shows how each characteristic effectively replaces the spirit of fear.

As our hearts beat with love for God and others, the results will soon show in our mouths. A spirit of love is evident in our speech in numerous ways.

Patience. Patient people refuse to carry out revenge even when they are able to do so. Patient words of forgiveness, understanding, and love seek to restore relationships that are in jeopardy. Patient words genuinely speak to the welfare and prosperity of our adversaries (Matthew 5:43–48; Romans 12:17–21).

Kindness. Kind words reflect a sensitivity to the problems, positions, and responsibilities of others. Kindness unfolds in questions that seek to genuinely understand and in expressions that are soft, gentle, and encouraging.

Lack of envy. If we have genuine love for others, we are thrilled to see them prosper, and our words reflect our feelings. Yet many of us find it hard to tell someone else, "Good job," "Congratulations," "We are happy for you," or "You deserve it." We may find it even harder to *feel* glad that God chose to bless someone other than us.

Lack of boasting. A loving spirit gives God credit for accomplishments and gains.

Humility. A truly humble person admits when he or she is wrong, gives God credit for any personal gain, and speaks words of glad submission to Christ.

Concern for others. A loving heart is not self-seeking, but is concerned about things of interest and importance to others. A genuinely concerned person silently listens to hear all that someone else has to say.

Slowness to anger. It's difficult to talk to some people because they are so easily angered. But people who are slow to anger are sought out by others. Those who can hold their tongues until hearing the whole story, and then ask pertinent questions, can usually formulate a wise evaluation and response.

No record of wrong. Divine love refuses to bring up previous (and supposedly forgiven) offenses. It never says, "I told you so." It has erased the tapes of the past and speaks only words of encouragement about the future.

No delight in evil. Love eliminates gossip, slander, or anything that communicates an evil report about another. It never encourages another person to do wrong and is never petty. It expresses grief and sorrow over anything contrary to God's righteousness and produces words that affirm faithful obedience.

Truth. All of these other characteristics are pointless if we don't deal in absolute truth. A heart filled with love results in words of truth as well as humility, kindness, concern, and so on.

Protection. Protective words respond to negative information by always giving others the benefit of the doubt. People who are being talked about may need an advocate, so we might use statements such as, "Are you sure you have all the facts?" or "I know that person, and I'd be surprised if that were really true." If the damaging statement does turn out to be true, protection says, "Let's tell no one else and pray for ways to constructively deal with this matter," or "Why don't we go hear this person's side of the story?"

Trust. A loving spirit results in verbal affirmations of trust in others. This is not the same as being foolishly naive or vulnerable. However, trust rejects words of suspicion, judgment, and doubt, and it promotes the integrity and virtue of another until the person is proven otherwise.

FEAR (Self-Centered)	LOVE'S TRANSFORMING QUALITY	LOVE (Others-Centered)
Lashes out to protect myself; fear of vulnerability	PATIENT	Trusts God to work in my offender's life while doing good to my offender
Thinks only of myself, being kind to "me" and expecting others to do the same	KIND	Looks at life from others' points of view and seeks to help them with an understanding spirit
Fears personal loss; compares and wonders why I don't have others' good fortune	NOT ENVIOUS	Rejoices in the prosperity of others, shares in their joy
Draws attention to myself; fears the loss of acclaim	NOT BOASTFUL	Focuses on God's goodness to me and the accomplishments of others
Fears a loss of status and prestige, does everything to put myself ahead	HUMBLE	Wants God to be truly first in my life and the lives of others
Looks out for my best interests and advantage with a strong focus on rights and privileges	NOT SELF-SEEKING	Looks out for the best interests of God and others
Is quick to defend my personal territory, dreams, and desires	NOT EASILY ANGERED	Hesitates and evaluates each situation from God's (and others') points of view
Remembers past offenses to use as ammunition in the future to defend, intimidate, or control	KEEPS NO RECORD OF WRONGS	Forgives for the sake of another and doesn't seek to control through past offenses

FEAR (Self-Centered)	LOVE'S TRANSFORMING QUALITY	LOVE (Others-Centered)
Uses evil schemes and words to protect and enhance personal position and personal gain	TAKES NO DELIGHT IN EVIL	Recognizes that evil is always harmful to everyone involved; is willing to refrain for the sake of God and others
Recognizes the value of truth only when it is convenient, often lies to protect self or gain advantage	REJOICES IN THE TRUTH	Recognizes the value of truth, even if it means admitting to wrongdoing
In order to protect self, is willing to endanger others both spiritually and physically	PROTECTS	Desires to shelter others from danger, even at cost to self
Is suspicious, doubtful, and skeptical, especially in situations that threaten some kind of personal loss	TRUSTS	Willingly trusts in others until proven untrustworthy; seeks to engender trust
Discourages and belittles others' potential, fearing their gain at the expense of personal position or status	HOPES	Believes in the potential of others and encourages them to discover their potential even if it is personally threatening
Stops loving as soon as it becomes too difficult, undeserved, or inconvenient; fears becoming used or taken advantage of	PERSEVERES	Loves regardless of external circumstances or the worthiness of the person

Hope. The hopeful aspect of love projects an optimistic vision for the future. It speaks of positive worth and value, the solution of crises, and the eventual resolution of problems. It affirms that we can do all things through Christ's strength (Philippians 4:13).

Perseverance. Divine love endures regardless of the circumstances. It allows us to express words of love toward enemies. It helps us continue to show concern for others even during times of extended personal crises. It's the quality that helps love endure even while under pressure.

There is no better model of commitment to a blended "trust-love" life demonstrated in words than the example of Jesus Christ. In the depths of the greatest personal crisis of His life, Jesus trusted His Father and focused on the needs of others (1 Peter 2:21–25). Even while hanging on the cross, His words showed concern for others. He asked forgiveness for His persecutors (Luke 23:34). He instructed John to take care of His mother (John 19:26–27). He proclaimed, "It is finished" (v. 30) for all the world to hear, speaking of His work of love in dying for us. We are challenged to develop the same mind-set and faith in God that motivated Christ Jesus (Philippians 2:5).

A commitment to trust and love dispels the failure of fearful speech and transforms our words into verbal bouquets of grace, concern, and encouragement. Enjoy the fearless beauty of entwining trust and love in your heart, and share the joy with others through your words.

12

APPLES OF GOLD

A Commitment to Positive Speech

A story reported in 1996 told of a retired eighty-five-year-old man who used to frequent a Kroger supermarket in Georgia. He was described as "sort of a mean old man" and "bossy and very particular about things." He had breakfast in the store every morning, and sometimes on hot summer days he wouldn't bother to wear a shirt or shoes. He often frowned, grumbled, and commented on how the female clerks in the store were overweight.

A few weeks after the old man died of cancer, another man came into the store and began handing out $10,000 checks to several of the clerks. The financial adviser for the old man, he explained that his client had gotten to know the ladies pretty well and thought they could probably use the money. What had they done to merit such a gift? *They had talked to him!* Even when the man had been cranky and insulting, they had still spoken pleasantly to him and treated him well. They even visited him in the hospital after he got sick. The clerks thought they were just being neighborly. None of them expected anything in return and were shocked to receive checks from the man's estate.

Our pleasant words don't always result in such a tangible payoff. Yet God's Word highlights many rewards for those who use their speech to bless others. The productive tongue is characterized as being wise, like choice silver, a banquet for many, the Lord's delight, a guardian of the soul, a vehicle to turn away wrath, a healer, a tree of life, full of knowledge, and a reflection of faithfulness (Proverbs 10:19–21; 12:22; 13:3; 15:1, 4; 17:27; 31:26). In fact, the proper use of our words is compared to "apples of gold in settings of silver" (25:11).

It is challenging to develop positive speech patterns in a world that has become insensitive to God's perspectives of proper talk. However, maintaining three important commitments will guard the sacredness of your words and help you become a better example for others: (1) developing your own spiritual maturity; (2) speaking only good things about other people; and (3) responding properly whenever you encounter improper speech habits.

A COMMITMENT TO MATURITY

Your foremost commitment should be to nurture and protect the development of humility, patience, and love. These are qualities that grow over a lifetime. They are taught by the Spirit through His Word and grafted into your life by attentive application and continued commitment.

Here are a few suggestions to help you better incorporate the qualities of love, patience, and humility into your everyday life.

Define these terms in your own words. Be as precise and practical as you can in determining what you want humility, patience, and love to mean to you. Make your definitions concise, biblical, interesting, and relevant. Be creative.

Memorize your definitions and relevant Scripture passages. Use repetition and memorization to fortify your sensitivity to the essence and importance of genuine humility, patience, and love.

Pray regularly for the Spirit to develop each of the three areas. Prayer will not only unleash the Spirit's work, but it will also help remind you of your commitment. It is likely that most people will need to pray several times a day.

Speak less and listen more. Allow the principles of humility, patience, and love to guard your lips. David prayed, "Set a guard, O Lord, over my mouth; keep watch over the door of my lips" (Psalm 141:3).

Evaluate frequently. Your goal is to live by your newly established standards, not the lower criteria of the world.

Be patient. Your spirit and your speech will not be transformed in a day. Patiently persist!

A COMMITMENT TO ONLY POSITIVE REPORTS

After hearing something scandalous about someone else, our natural response is to perpetuate the news in the form of slander, gossip, murmuring, or beguilement. This results not in the restoration of the offender, but rather in his alienation. It's not long until he feels that everyone is against him. Seeds of resentment and bitterness take root in his heart that drive a wedge between him and his fellow believers. Occasionally, someone will sense the person is being mistreated and rally to his cause. Yet rather than solving the problem, this frequently results in God's people choosing sides and waging a divisive war.

Therefore, we must be committed to saying only good things about others. When problems arise that make this difficult to do, Jesus instructs us how to respond. Implementing this process protects our newfound joy of having a tongue in check. It makes reconciliation more likely and less risky. When you're tempted to perpetuate negative information about someone, you can choose a God-honoring path by following the five steps found in Matthew 18:15–17:

1. *Recognize our "familyship"* (Matthew 18:15). At a family gathering, one of my young nieces blurted out, "Daddy, isn't this good familyship?" She was already aware of a special bond between family members. The same is true of a Christian "family," who share a special oneness in Christ. Our unity calls for living, protecting, supporting, and helping one another. When a Christian brother or sister sins, we are to respond with love and acceptance. Our bond in Christ needs to be an undeniable reality that prompts love for one another. It's a family affair.

In this context, it is significant that Christ said, "If your *brother* sins . . ." Some of us tolerate a lot from blood relatives but are quite insensitive to members of our Christian family. If there is anything to our Christianity, we must attempt to heal, support, and love those who are hurting in our extended Christian family (John 13:34–35). If we are unwilling to accept our family responsibilities, we will verbally destroy each other.

2. *Gain a clear perception of the problem* (Matthew 18:15). Sometimes we are hard on people who haven't actually sinned. If it is not clear-cut that a fellow Christian has actually committed a sin, we should ask several questions: *Am I being overly sensitive? Have I obtained sufficient facts? Is this firsthand information or has it been passed down the rumor mill? Does this offense actually violate scriptural teaching, or does it just conflict with my own opinions and preconceptions? Am I responding negatively because of a previous offense?*

With these questions in mind, our hearts will be open to a clear understanding of the situation. Too often we write people off quickly and don't bother to give them an opportunity to explain or defend themselves. Yet no final conclusions should be reached until the next step is taken.

3. *Demonstrate God's love to the person* (Matthew 18:15). This step has three important elements that apply to conscientious Christians eager to bring negative talk to an end.

- *Take the initiative.* Many problems continue to exist between Christians because of apathy or lethargy. Yet we need to remember that when we sin and weaken our relationship with God, He takes the initiative to approach us (Genesis 3; John 3:16). Therefore, whenever we see someone trapped in a verbal sin cycle, we too ought to be willing to approach the person with the intent of restoring him or her.

  Our approach should be preceded by prayer that God will provide the right opportunity, and then we need to be sensitive to His timing. And according to Galatians 6:1, we must be spiritual (in fellowship and in harmony with God), gentle (without inner bitterness, revenge, or hostility), and cautious. In our desire to help the other person, we must take care lest, in the process, we also fall into sin.

- *Show the other person his or her fault.* This must be done lovingly and carefully. We must consistently convey love through our attitudes and words to avoid a judgmental, "holier than thou" attitude. It is also essential to listen carefully with an open mind to determine the facts, the other person's point of view, and his or her attitudes (defensive, hostile, repentant, proud).

- *Keep the matter between the two of you.* When you have a problem with someone, you go to that person *first.* Otherwise, you drag other people into the conflict prematurely, and perhaps needlessly. If you can assure the other person you have discussed this issue with no one else, you'll benefit from the trust that results.

    If a fellow Christian responds, he or she is restored to God's fellowship and to ours. The problem should then be forgotten—separated "as far as the east is from the west" (Psalm 103:12). If, however, the person will not settle the matter, and if the offense warrants further attention, we can move on to the next step in Christ's instructions.

4. *Demonstrate God's love with one or two others* (Matthew 18:16). If we have prayerfully concluded that we are correct in the matter and our one-on-one encounter with the offending person doesn't work, we should return with one or two carefully chosen people. We must select well-qualified people who won't take sides, who are respected by the offending party, and who share our goal of loving restoration. It is also helpful if these companions have been through the same problem as the offender so that they can provide experience and assure him of potential victory.

The purpose of this step is to restore the offender and establish the truth of the situation in the presence of impartial witnesses. If the offender still refuses to respond to the love of his brothers, the matter should be taken to the church.

5. *Demonstrate God's love through the church* (Matthew 18:17). For serious matters in which the offending party shows no remorse, you may need to approach your church leadership (pastor or official board) and lovingly discuss with them the sin problem you have attempted to restore. Take along the individuals who have confronted the offender with you. The church leadership should hear the matter and make their recommendation. If they agree that the offending person is wrong, yet he does not respond to this attempt at restoration, then he is to be released from the fellowship of the church.

Our goal should be for all our conversations to be filled with good reports about one another. When bad reports creep in from time to time, they should be dealt with as quickly and as sensitively as possible. Rather than passing along negative information, it should be limited to just the few who play a part in the solution and the restoration of the person in question. Positive conversation produces gratefulness toward each other, a spirit of joy, and a stimulation to grow in the Lord.

I can think of only a few exceptions to this guideline. God's Word states that two people in a husband/wife relationship are as one. Though there may be times when we don't wish to burden our partners with negative information, their counsel and prayer support will be a valuable resource. However, both husband and wife must share the commitments of confidentiality and a Spirit-controlled tongue.

Some situations will require special insight and perspective, and the need for someone else's godly advice may be necessary. God's Word reminds us that there is wisdom in a multitude of counselors (Proverbs 11:14). But during such times we should seek a neutral counselor unaware of the situation or the people involved. It is essential to preserve the anonymity of those involved and protect their reputations.

During New Testament times, church leaders frequently warned about false teachers and individuals who would hurt the assembly if they were not exposed. Similar situations may come up from time to time today. But whenever it becomes necessary to speak out against someone, it should be done as it was in Scripture: specific details of the sin are not shared, and it is done with tears (1 Timothy 1:18–20; Philippians 3:18–19).

CONSTRUCTIVE RESPONSES

Our third commitment should be to respond to negative input without making the situation worse. The previous section outlined what to do when we know or hear something negative about a fellow Christian. But learning to properly respond to the verbal sins we encounter in everyday conversation is crucial to our continued growth. How do we answer those whose speech is not up to the standards we have set for ourselves?

According to Proverbs 15:28, "The heart of the righteous ponders how to answer, but the mouth of the wicked pours out evil things." As we think back through our commitments, we can "ponder" seven ways in which we can wisely respond to improper speech.

1. *Do not communicate approval of what is being said or encourage additional statements about the matter* (1 Thessalonians 5:15, 22; 1 Timothy 5:22). Encouragement can be communicated both verbally and physically. Even if we don't approve of what is being said, we might nod our heads to show that we are listening. However, a nod of the head may be interpreted as agreement and will allow the sin to continue. Even if what the person shares is true, we must not give the impression that we condone his violation of a biblical principle. It is better to quietly listen with neither verbal nor nonverbal response until we have an opportunity to interject a change in the course of the conversation.

2. *Pray for wisdom* (James 1:5–7). While you are listening, send up a quick prayer for wisdom. During the course of the encounter, you will be surprised how God helps you.

3. *Respond in the context of your own commitments.* Communicate truthfully but with love. Keep your focus on God's perspective in the matter. Don't forget that God cares about the well-being of the one spoken about, as well as the speaker. By

patiently hesitating, evaluating, and resisting the sins of anger, you will help turn the focus to God and a loving resolution. Encourage the one who shares the information to look for ways to meet the needs of the one he speaks about. And don't forget your commitment to share only positive information about others.

4. *Avoid a judgmental spirit* (Galatians 5:22; 6:1). Be sure to communicate love in every statement you make. A judgmental or rude spirit will only alienate the other person and make it impossible to lead him or her to the joy of a Spirit-controlled tongue.

5. *Encourage other people to control their tongues.* The best time to act is before the person has time to spread negative information about someone else. When someone is about to tell you a juicy tidbit, it's easy to listen to what they have to say before you begin to be concerned. But a better option is to say, "Don't tell me. I already have more negative thoughts than I know what to do with."

Many times at social gatherings someone will get just far enough into a story to have everyone's attention and then say, "You know, I really shouldn't be telling you this." And of course the listeners all respond, "Oh, come on, you can't stop now! We won't tell." It would be refreshing to hear someone respond instead, "Good for you. Don't tell. I admire your self-control." We need to do what we can to stop negative talk before it gets spread.

6. *Pray about what you hear* (Philippians 4:6–7; 1 Peter 5:7). When you can't avoid hearing a disparaging report about someone, pray for healing, conviction, growth, reconciliation, wisdom, or whatever is appropriate. As you pray, God will direct your responses.

7. *Publicly share your commitment to a Spirit-controlled tongue.* The best way to avoid the embarrassment of being party to an uncontrolled tongue is to control your tongue and let others know of your commitment. Tactfully share your commitment with your family, friends, and church. Ask them to patiently encourage you and pray for you. As other people become

aware of your desire to control your tongue, they will become sensitive not to share inappropriate information with you.

Nurturing our inner maturity, restricting our conversation to good reports, and being constructive in the face of negative input will not only fortify and stimulate our growth, but it will infect others with an awareness of the positive benefit of a tongue in check!

Words fitly spoken are like apples of gold in settings of silver—a tree of life to all who hear (Proverbs 25:11; 15:4). They are the Lord's delight!

STUDY GUIDE

by

James S. Bell Jr.

Chapter One
A WORD'S WORTH

1. Recall a time when you were unsure of yourself, and the power of someone's words helped you to succeed. What positive role did those words play?

2. Now think back to when you had basic confidence in your abilities and someone criticized you. If it contributed to your failure, what negative role did it play?

3. You stumble because something is blocking your path. When have your words obstructed someone's progress and caused hurt in the process?

4. One small, single word can upset an entire relationship or situation. Can you identify when misunderstood words (or ones meant to hurt) had devastating results? Why?

5. Even godly people can criticize the faults of others. How do negative things shared in a spiritual context sometimes go against the Christian principles those same people espouse?

6. Like a frog in the kettle, we can slowly get used to a harmful situation with increasing negative effects. When have you finally woken up to speech patterns that were damaging you or others?

Chapter Two
TO TELL THE TRUTH

1. How are Mark Twain's words especially true in today's society
   —that telling the truth will confound your enemies and
   astound your friends? When have you been in this type of
   situation?

2. What situations can you think of where lying has actually
   been represented as a virtue? Why is the truth more important than the supposed "good" resulting from the lie?

3. In what ways have you lied in the past to gain advantage,
   protection, or promotion of personal interests? Though it
   may have seemed to work at first, what did you sacrifice?

4. In your past what types of lies have been premeditated as opposed to those which were spontaneous? What does this say to you about deeply ingrained sin of which you may not have been aware?

5. Set aside time to pray for wisdom in your speech, especially in the gray areas where truth is required but silence and discretion may be further assets. Write down principles for different circumstances.

6. Which of the following "gray" areas do you struggle with the most in terms of truth: compliments, withholding information, or protecting others? Where do you tend to cross the line with supposed good intentions?

Chapter Three
MALICIOUSLY SPEAKING

1. If gossip and slander focus on someone else entirely, how can they be vehicles to promote self? Why do many insecure people suffer from these sins?

2. Explain why sloth and slander are linked. Has there been a relationship between the "slower" times in your life and the temptation to get *too* involved in the lives of others?

3. Check your own heart to determine when you have been bitter or resentful toward others. In what cases has this caused you to speak maliciously in order to pay them back?

4. Gossips often fail to keep secrets. How much do you value the word *confidential* in your relationships? Under what circumstances are you tempted to betray confidences and rationalize it?

5. Isolate a damaging case of slander. Be specific in terms of how it adversely affected each of the three people involved —the speaker, the listener, and the subject.

6. Because of the long-term devastating consequences of slander, even if you were only the listener, take at least one of the four options listed by the author in accordance with God's Word to rectify the situation.

Chapter Four
THE EGO IN OUR MOUTHS

1. What areas of your ego at times go beyond the bounds of caring properly for yourself and making the most of your talents for God? How might these occasions of pride lead to the sins of the tongue mentioned in this chapter?

2. Of three forms of boasting—vain conceit, bragging, and taking another's credit—which are you most susceptible to and why? Also, what lessons has God taught you as you've overcome any or all of the above?

3. Why is salvation in Christ a completely humbling experience? Why do we want to play a role and help God out? Show how this relates to the way we speak about ourselves.

4. How does flattery differ from genuine and appropriate compliments? We often feel we can do no harm in praising others. Yet are there motives for a return benefit? Seek a pure and generous heart in praising others.

5. Exaggeration can be associated with many purposes—to entertain or manipulate others, or for personal gain. Ask someone to monitor everything you say over the next week to measure how you might stray from the exact truth in various areas.

6. Because exaggeration erodes trust and credibility and may sometimes be an unconscious act, seek honesty from others in your home and workplace. Ask for examples so you may correct this pervasive sin.

Chapter Five
CROSS WORDS

1. Rank in order, from the greatest to the least, the root causes for your murmuring and contentious words: anger, irritation, disappointment, impatience, stress, insecurity, and guilt.

2. Now analyze your top three choices. Do they tend to be the areas of character weakness you battle with on the whole? Claim the promises of God to give you more of the character of Christ through the power of His Spirit.

3. A murmuring spirit often begins with one person and affects the entire environment. Identify times when the end product included one or more of the author's eight negative results. What does this teach you about this seemingly harmless habit?

4. Consider an unacceptable or unfair situation in your life in the recent past or present. Spell out two different approaches: (1) a typical process of murmuring in reaction; (2) the constructive steps of prayer, and approaching the proper authority. How will the outcomes be different?

5. It's hard to identify division in our midst. In what form might contention be found among those around you? Make an agreement to put others' concerns first, as well as a commitment to encouragement and edification. How might this affect the spirit of your disagreements?

6. Locate a positive role model, someone who has been effective in overcoming a contentious spirit in others. What was the secret of his success? Make a commitment to follow his example.

Chapter Six
EXPLETIVES DELETED

1. In what ways have you devalued God's name by speaking of Him as less than He is: through complaining, blame, unbelief, or even a faulty theology? Study God's attributes and pinpoint where your words have brought Him down to your level.

2. Do a study of the names of God. The best way is to choose an existing collection from Scripture with a commentary. Look particularly at the names that emphasize His holiness and our need for reverence and healthy fear.

3. When has God's name been a strong tower for you—when you've employed it for protection, comfort, growth, or evangelism? How has that caused you to greater revere His power and majesty?

4. Look at the last ten years of your life. How have the influences of the relativistic culture, especially the media, desensitized you to sensuous language? What do you tolerate now that you wouldn't ten years ago?

5. Have a discussion with your family and other believers with whom you fellowship regarding what qualifies as foolish talk, coarse jesting, or vulgarity. Be willing to conform to God's strict standards rather than society's rationalizations.

6. When you hear coarse speech of any kind, pray about practicing the habit of countering it by giving God glory in some tangible way. This will work better than direct criticism or judgment.

Chapter Seven
HEART TALK

1. If the tongue is the servant of the heart, why is it that we can deceive others by saying what we don't really believe? If we can only put on an act for so long, how are we eventually exposed?

2. When, even without intending it, has your tongue been an open grave, producing death—discouragement, pessimism, ridicule, sarcasm? What connected area of your heart contains a "graveyard"—desires, attitudes, or beliefs not linked to the life of God?

3. Now review the many times your words have been a fountain of life to others, producing multiple blessings evidenced in their lives. What connected areas of your heart are like a well-watered garden stemming from prayer, worship, good deeds, or time in God's Word?

4. Anger needs to be dealt with constructively because many of the sins of the tongue have a root in anger. Yet you must first find out what makes you angry. Is it frustrations, bitterness, fear, or insecurity? Make a further list and attach circumstances. Seek to rectify these issues.

5. What are your greatest fears? Are you on a self-survival track to cope with and manage them? Does your tongue betray those fears in various ways? Pray now to put your fears in the hands of an all-powerful God who tells you to cast your burdens on Him.

6. One way to deal with your pride is to see in 1 Samuel 2:3 that God is aware of our thoughts and words and weighs them. See your accomplishments in light of His perfect words and deeds in order to achieve true humility.

Chapter Eight
SPEAKING OUT FOR NUMBER ONE

1. Just as cutting in line is a sign of self-priority, so are other signs of our culture, such as divorce. Make a list of selfish trends that put self-advancement above the needs of others. Are there any patterns you can describe?

2. In the areas of legalism and personal freedom related to issues not completely spelled out in the Scriptures, there is often a pride component going in either direction. Check your own attitudes. Do you feel superior in terms of your point of view or behavior?

3. Counterfeit humility is actually a form of pride and may be unintentional. List as many forms of incomplete humility as you can think of—the worst being the attempt to draw attention to how humble you are!

4. God may wish us to live with certain weaknesses, as the apostle Paul did. Do you glory in your weaknesses? Ask God to clearly show you how He is glorified in your weaknesses as you yield to Him.

5. Suffering presents you with a choice—resist its lessons or learn humility. Take three instances of suffering in your own life and write out both how you grew in humility as well as lessons you could have learned but either refused or didn't understand.

6. God exalts those who humble themselves before Him, that is, those who look out for Him as "number one" in their lives. In what ways has God exalted you as you have made Him your first priority instead of yourself?

Chapter Nine
DEFUSING ANGER

1. Unjust anger may assume very different manifestations and consequences. Look at the difference between Jonah's and Cain's anger. Compare their stories to how you usually respond to God with your anger.

2. Anger and impatience are closely related. Reflect on a situation where one led to the other in your own life. How can you better seek God's grace to overcome an impatient spirit in order to diffuse anger at the source?

3. When has legitimate anger worked on your behalf? Whether it's injustice toward someone else or our sin within, we need to be deeply roused to action.

4. When are you perhaps not angry enough in the face of sin or injustice? Some anger relates to deep hurt or abuse of the past. Whether it's you or someone close to you, seek forgiveness and healing. Allow these hurts to be expressed without dwelling on them.

5. There are many ways to slow down the anger process. Review the author's five suggestions and identify the one that would probably be the most helpful to you (or already is). Then, name the one you least often employ. Why is that the case?

6. The author lists ten sources of anger and how to apply patience to them. Take the three that present the biggest challenge in your life. Besides merely applying the solution for patience, find specific instances in your past related to these three areas and reconcile where possible.

Chapter Ten
PATIENCE APPLIED

1. Sometimes anger seems unexplainable. An alarm goes off, and you go out of control. Whether fear, pride, or some other sin pattern that may be deep but not fully recognized, ask God to reveal the source of unexplained extreme reactions.

2. Sometimes anger focuses on a seemingly impossible person or unsolveable problem and creates an endless round of distraction. Describe your pattern of mental dialogue that never resolves the issue but does deplete energy. Pray that God will give you grace to deal with it.

3. Consider your greatest area of recurring anger. Similar to the story of the husband late for dinner, write out your pattern of the "fret-envy-anger-wrath-evil" syndrome. Provide solutions at each step of the way. If your cycle still goes all the way to evil, how can you make amends?

4. Try a hypothetical situation: imagine your fret mode regarding the above problem. Now reread the descriptions of the "trust-delight-commit-rest-wait patiently" solution. Apply these principles on a piece of paper at every level of the anger syndrome.

5. Patience is also the willingness to carefully go all the way with the proper reactions toward anger. Forgiveness, honesty, and proper action are the most important. All require carefully chosen words. Where do the right words fail you the most? Ask God to teach you in this area.

6. The right response with the best words is critical in rectifying anger. Ask God for the wisdom and knowledge behind the words that must come first—and ask Him how to express those words diplomatically and with courtesy and honesty.

Chapter Eleven
THE TRUST-LOVE LIFE

1. Has your fear ever acted in ways that actually helped that fear to become a reality? For example, fearing others' displeasure causes behavior that only increases their displeasure. Think of other examples, and discover ways to change.

2. Name your fears in situations where you failed God in your duty. Relate it to your lack of trust in God's power to overcome circumstances or your weaknesses. Has God ever truly failed you? On the other hand, look at His marvelous provision and deliverance.

3. At times fear is justified—if we have sinned or are out of God's will. When have you sinned and your fears came true? On the other hand, God protects us even when we sin. In what ways has He kept you from even worse harm when you've walked out of His will?

4. A trusting heart has no need for the sins of the tongue. Look at the author's eight bullet points and write next to each on another piece of paper a practical way to fulfill that good, either in an actual present situation or a hypothetical future one.

5. Read through 1 Corinthians 13 once every day for the next week to have a clear picture of what it means to have a loving spirit. Write an insight on each of those seven days regarding a different aspect of love and try to put it into practice on that day.

6. On the "heart-level love" chart in this chapter, where do you find your biggest challenge to love linked to one of your major fears? Here's your opportunity to link a direct solution to a direct problem. The next time you face the fear, directly apply the love factor.

Chapter Twelve
APPLES OF GOLD

1. All your words should be sacred; as it says in Scripture, we should speak the "oracles of God." Measure your words over the next day and see how they live up to God's Word. Though every word may not be spiritual, how God-honoring are they?

2. Make a point of spreading a good report about someone you may have been less than charitable to in the past. One way to do this is to find a recent accomplishment that has been largely unnoticed by others. Share this with those who can in turn respond to that person positively.

3. Most believers have experienced an offense from another believer that requires the process of Matthew 18—go to him; expose the fault; show God's love to others; and finally, go to the church. Seek to implement Matthew 18 with serious wrongs to yourself or others.

4. When you are exposed to conversation that is not God-honoring how would you rate your response: (1) often approving, (2) occasionally approving, (3) neutral, (4) bringing in a God-honoring perspective?

5. On the extreme side, we can be judgmental or condescending in response to words that are not God-honoring and cause others to stumble because of our spiritual superiority. Check your own behavior to measure where spiritual pride may have come into play.

6. Finally, make a decision to share with those closest to you, your commitment to a Spirit-controlled tongue. Communicate the principles found in this book and share with others how your speech patterns (and the heart behind it) are being transformed by the power of God.